NAVIGATING THE STORMS

NAVIGATING THE STORMS

Leading Christian Schools with Character and Conviction

Kenneth S. Coley, EdD

purposeful design.
PUBLICATIONS

Colorado Springs, Colorado

Purposeful Design Publications is the publishing division of the Association of Christian Schools International (ACSI) and is committed to the ministry of Christian school education, to enable Christian educators and schools worldwide to effectively prepare students for life. As the publisher of textbooks, trade books, and other educational resources within ACSI, Purposeful Design Publications strives to produce biblically sound materials that reflect Christian scholarship and stewardship and that address the identified needs of Christian schools around the world.

The views expressed in this publication are those of the author, and they may not necessarily represent the position of the Association of Christian Schools International.

Unless otherwise identified, all Scripture quotations are taken from the New American Standard Bible®. Copyright © 1960, 1962, 1963, 1968, 1971, 1972, 1973, 1975, 1977, 1995 by The Lockman Foundation. Used by permission.

Scripture quotations marked (ESV) are taken from The Holy Bible, English Standard Version® (ESV®). Copyright © 2001 by Crossway, a publishing ministry of Good News Publishers. Used by permission. All rights reserved.

Scripture quotations marked (HCSB) are taken from the Holman Christian Standard Bible®. Copyright © 2003, 2002, 2000, 1999 by Holman Bible Publishers. All rights reserved.

Scripture quotations marked (KJV) are taken from the King James Version (KJV).

Scripture quotations marked (NIV) are taken from the Holy Bible, New International Version®, NIV®. Copyright © 1973, 1978, 1984 by Biblica, Inc.™ Used by permission of Zondervan. All rights reserved worldwide. www.zondervan.com

Scripture quotations marked (NKJV) are taken from the Holy Bible, New King James Version (NKJV). Copyright © 1982 by Thomas Nelson, Inc. Used by permission. All rights reserved.

Scripture quotations marked The Message are taken from The Message. Copyright © 1993, 1994, 1995, 1996, 2000, 2001, 2002. Used by permission of NavPress Publishing Group.

Sample Streamlined Contractual Faith-Based Employment Dispute Resolution Program by Mediation Law Group Resources. Reprinted with permission of Mediation Law Group Inc.

Policies on student use of cell phones and personal websites used by permission of Christian Law Association.

Printed in the United States of America
19 18 17 16 15 14 13 12 11   2 3 4 5 6 7

Library of Congress Cataloging-in-Publication Data

Coley, Kenneth S., 1952-
    Navigating the storms : leading Christian schools with character and conviction / Kenneth S. Coley.
        p. cm.
    Includes bibliographical references.
    ISBN 978-1-58331-351-0 (pbk.)
    1. Church schools--United States--Administration. 2. School management and organization--United States. 3. Educational leadership--United States. I. Title.
    LC368.C66 2010
    371.071'068--dc22
                                        2010029668

Catalog #6623

Designer: Mike Riester
Editorial team: Christina Reidl, Cheryl Chiapperino, John Conaway

Purposeful Design Publications
A Division of ACSI
PO Box 65130 • Colorado Springs, CO 80962-5130
Customer Service: 800-367-0798 • www.acsi.org

To Scott and Caitlin ...

Many times my son and daughter have encouraged me by living out
the leadership principles described in these pages.

Kathy and I praise God for them. In the words of the apostle Paul,
they are truly "His workmanship" (Ephesians 2:10, NKJV).
And we thank our God "upon every remembrance" of them (Philippians 1:3).

Contents

Foreword

In my first position as principal, I was serving at a newly created Christian school on the campus of a former military academy. The campus was in disrepair, so the summer before the opening of the school was very labor intensive. It was apparent that the school would not open in the fall unless we obtained help that was skilled in a variety of building and renovation areas—and soon!

Enter the Navigators, a Christian-based organization out of Colorado that had a local ministry among the military in San Diego. A partnership that allowed the Navigators to conduct training in the morning and provide skilled labor in the afternoon was formed. What once seemed overwhelmingly impossible was now possible. School opened on time in the fall. The same partnership was used the following summer as well. In honor of this gargantuan service rendered, the school's first mascot was named the Navigator, symbolized by a seaman behind the wheel of a ship. Incidentally, the school was set on a hill overlooking the Pacific Ocean, so the Navigator was definitely an appropriate mascot name.

Using a navigator as a metaphor in a book on Christian school administration is also appropriate. The picture of a *helmsman*, or a *pilot*, steering a ship is a clear image of the essential significance of the administrator who steers a Christian school— and that very image is the premise for this book.

Dr. Ken Coley follows his highly practical leadership book *The Helmsman: Leading with Courage and Wisdom* with this book, *Navigating the Storms: Leading Christian Schools with Character and Conviction*. It is an excellent sequel, especially considering our current days and times. Christian schools have perhaps never faced a more vulnerable and dangerous voyage as they navigate the storms of life and of our culture.

A biblical foundation is quickly established as the author introduces the Greek word that Paul used in 1 Corinthians 12:28 for *administrations*, one of the gifts from the Holy Spirit. The verb form of the word means "to steer," and, in yet another form, the word refers to a person who pilots a ship. Dr. Coley has certainly chosen an apt key word to steer the direction of his book!

The first section of the book, "The Mindscape of the Helmsman," describes the inner life and preparation necessary for the administrator to become as effective as possible. In a conversational style, the author weaves nautical stories into the teaching of each administrative concept. The product of such crucibles as "wreckers" and "ledges" is the perfecting of the spirit, mind, will, emotions, and attitude of the Christian school leader. This perfecting process should result in strength of character exemplified by high integrity and more-mature faith.

The author capably illustrates this inner-core growth in a number of ways. First, Dr. Coley gives examples of Christian school realities that would test the mettle of any administrator. Second, he cites scriptural models that give great credence to the character God wants to build in each of His children. Third, he uses the nautical metaphor to present clear problems from history that offered helmsmen the opportunity to mature in their inner person. Fourth, he introduces research from reputable sources that highlights what works or doesn't work in regard to the mindscape of the helmsman.

The main characteristic that exemplifies a strong, mature mindscape is integrity. Tied to integrity are words like *soundness, wholeness, purity,* and *incorruption.* Having integrity can allow a leader to have a vibrant "faith and a good conscience, which some have rejected and suffered shipwreck in regard to their faith" (1 Timothy 1:19).

The second section is "The Skills of the Helmsman." Here Dr. Coley places a special emphasis on the skills of mentoring; managing change; dismissing staff and students, and being dismissed yourself; and vitally important, relating well, as the school's chief administrator, to the school board. Once again the author illustrates and applies leadership skills by employing practical Christian school examples, nautical-culture narratives, biblical models, and leadership research selections.

Anyone who is currently involved in Christian school leadership or is even contemplating a future in this arena will benefit from adding this book to his or her professional library. It is practical and biblical as it mentors leaders in *navigating storms* and *leading Christian schools with character and conviction.*

Randall A. Ross, EdD
Regional Director
ACSI Ohio River Valley Region

Acknowledgments

At the completion of a project like this, I am deeply aware of the significant contributions that so many people have made to craft and launch this book. Giving thanks to the Lord, I wish to recognize the following:

+ My wife, Kathy, for her continued commitment to my ministry and her insights into the issues with which the Lord has called me to wrestle. She participates in almost daily rehearsal and review of my research and writing.

+ My colleague Daniel Heimbach (U.S. Naval Academy class of 1972) at Southeastern Baptist Theological Seminary for his coaching in all things nautical.

+ My good friend Dirk Mroczek, who is a Christian school administrator, for spending a marvelous fall day with me on the Chesapeake Bay and trusting me at the helm of his nineteen-foot sailboat.

+ David Edgell and the members of his church in Gloucester, Virginia, for giving Kathy and me a daylong outing at the mouth of the York River on a forty-footer. All administrators should experience the exhilaration of sailing and observing dolphin schools.

+ Three very gifted people—Currie Tilley, Phyllis Jackson, and Mindy Patton— for working tirelessly with me in the preparation of drafts and presentations.

+ Kelly Bennett and the Mediation Law Group for allowing me to include their material.

+ Christian Law Association for permitting me to use its policies on student use of cell phones and personal websites.

+ Steve Babbitt, the director of Publishing Services at Purposeful Design, for leading the editing and design team. Christina Reidl and Cheryl Chiapperino are exceptional at the craft of editing and "wordsmithing."

+ And finally, so many educators and leaders who have met me along the journey and expressed appreciation for some insight that has helped them in ministry. I marvel at the mysterious way the Lord allows writer and reader to connect for the benefit of both and to His glory.

NAVIGATING THE STORMS

A Word from the Author...

WHY ALL THE NAUTICAL STUFF?

After twenty-two years as a teacher, a coach, and a school administrator, I was given a special opportunity to continue my career as a Christian educator in a new setting—graduate school. While preparing lectures on school administration, I discovered in the writings of Kenn Gangel, Leonard Sweet, and others the helmsman concept behind the word that the apostle Paul selected when he discussed the *gift of administration*. In Paul's day, when his readers and hearers encountered the Greek word *kybernetes* (a form of *kybernesis*, used in 1 Corinthians 12:28), they connected it with the ordinary use of that word— a *helmsman*, or a *pilot* of a ship—because of their familiarity with sea travel. *Effectively leading and managing a group of believers* is analogous to steering a ship. It requires the skillful leadership of someone at the helm, someone who is charged with keeping the ship on course and ensuring the safety of all the passengers and the cargo.

Through discussing this concept with many leaders and educators, I realized that the word the Holy Spirit had inspired Paul to write provides a compelling picture for twenty-first-century leaders. In this word picture is a powerful metaphor capturing the challenges and crises that are standard fare for those called to ministry. As a school leader, you are the helmsman, and the faculty, staff, and students are your crew. With this in mind, I have started each chapter with a nautical story that paints a picture of an extreme test a helmsman might face. By doing so, I hope to connect you to Paul's insight into the real-life storms that confront Christian leaders. I wish you Godspeed at the helm of your ministry.

Introduction

There was surprising ease to his stride as he entered the meeting room. Like a veteran seaman stepping onto the deck of his sailing ship, his presence brought an air of calm and confidence that was difficult to define but unmistakable, nonetheless. It couldn't have been his height because he was of average stature. Nor was it athletic arrogance or menacing intimidation, two qualities that are often mentioned as sources of personal power. His shoulders—yes, that's it— square, straight, relaxed. His facial features were not remarkable except in their openness that indicated a life of integrity and in the absence of taut muscles that come from the grip of worry. His jaw was set, and his chin was raised ever so slightly—prepared to lead or serve, whatever the situation called for. Even the most casual observer would have noticed his eyes—like facets of a diamond, there was the sparkle of joy; with a slight turn there was a glint like sunlight reflecting off steel; and another turn revealed a prism of tenderness and sensitivity seldom seen in one with so many burdens. Those eyes invited you into a heart of passion, courage, and determination, and for any who paused to ponder their depth, there was the mysterious sense of gazing into a deep spring, ever fresh and flowing.

And then he spoke, as one with authority. We all knew that the helmsman had arrived and it was time to set sail.

In the summer of 1972, I, like so many young men before me and so many since, experienced the exhilaration of sailing for the first time at a YMCA camp at the mouth of the Neuse River on the North Carolina coast. As counselors, we were given free time each day, and we often chose to spend that time on the river, learning the rudiments of handling a small Sailfish or Sunfish. For college students like me who had spent all their childhood on land except for going on the occasional rowboat outing at a lake or fighting waves at the beach with a small raft, there was something unique, even sublime, about these adventures on the tributary of a major river that emptied into the Atlantic Ocean.

Perhaps it was the salt spray, the rough tug of the sheet in my hands, the distinctive slapping of the sails on the mast on a breezy summer afternoon. But what I recall most was the feel of the rudder as I, the novice sailor, fought to balance the small boat in the battle between the elements of wind and current. The greatest thrill of all was when we counselors, like the carefree sailors in Winslow Homer's painting Breezing Up, *hiked the small craft to gain maximum momentum. Along with the adrenaline rush of the boat's speed, there was the inevitable risk of capsizing, which we often did, and with it the monstrous task to right and bail the little craft.*

Years later I would once again be a novice, and I would know the exhilaration of a different sort, that of placing my hands on the helm of a much-different vessel. As the young administrator of a growing Christian school in a Washington DC suburb, I felt once again the impact of elemental forces on the balance and direction of the deck on which I stood. But now the forces were spiritual, cultural, and organizational currents that threatened to capsize a fledgling school guided by a determined but inexperienced pilot.

The Holy Spirit inspired the apostle Paul to select a Greek word for the gift of administration (*kybernesis*) in 1 Corinthians 12:28 that, in another form (*kybernetes*), was used in his day to represent both the person who governs an organization and the one who pilots a ship.* Though I did not know of this biblical-nautical intersection in my early days as an administrator, I have vivid memories of the veracity of this dynamic that Paul describes in his selection of the nautical word. For those readers who share the experience of fighting to keep a ship from capsizing during their watch, who understand *navigating storms,* consider the account of the author of *Mayflower: A Story of Courage, Community, and War* during a reenactment voyage of crossing the Atlantic Ocean in the original *Mayflower:*

> In 1957, the crew members of the *Mayflower II*—a replica of the original vessel, built in Brixton, England—became the first mariners of the modern era to experience what it was like to ride out a gale in a Jacobean-era ship. Over the course of the first few weeks of the passage, they had discovered that the *Mayflower II's* boxy hull shape took some getting used to. At times, the motion in the high aft poop cabin became so violent that Captain Alan Villiers—one of the most experienced blue-water sailors in the world—feared that he might be flung out of his bunk. What this ship would do in survival conditions was a matter of deep concern to Villiers and his men.

---

*See Acts 27:11 and Revelation 18:17 and also the discussion of this concept on page 12 of *The Helmsman: Leading with Courage and Wisdom* (Coley 2006).

Toward the end of the voyage, a storm set in, forcing Villiers to do as Master Jones had done 337 years before. As the motion of the ship in the giant waves became intolerable, he decided he had no option but to lie ahull. The sails were furled, and everything on deck was tied down. Then, with considerable trepidation, Villiers ordered that the helm be secured to leeward. "This was the crucial test," Villiers wrote. "Would she lie that way, more or less quietly, with the windage of the high poop keeping her shoulder to the sea? Or would she just wallow hopelessly in the great troughs, threatening to roll her masts out? We didn't know. No one had tried the maneuver in a ship like that for maybe two centuries."

As soon as the ship's bow swung into the wind, a remarkable change came over the *Mayflower II*. Even though she was under bare poles in a howling gale, her slablike topsides functioned as a kind of wooden storm sail, magically steadying the ship's motion. Almost perfectly balanced, the *Mayflower II* sat like a contented duck amid the uproar of the storm. After being pounded unmercifully by the waves, the ship was finally at peace. "I reflected that the Pilgrim Fathers, who tossed through many such a wild night in Atlantic storms, at least knew tranquility in great gales," Villiers wrote. (Philbrick 2006, 31–32; italics in original)

That's it! *Tranquility in great gales*—this is my prayer for you as you consider what the Lord is calling you to in your ministry. As you ponder the nautical stories, literature on administration, some case studies taken from schools like yours, and, most important, the Scripture presented in these pages, it is my hope that you will know this tranquility and contentment while *navigating the storms*. The book contains two sections—"Part One: The Mindscape of the Helmsman" and "Part Two: The Skills of the Helmsman." At the core of each section is the acknowledgment that leaders must be prepared for rough seas, first in their minds and hearts. We begin with the symbolism of lighthouses that both allow leaders to plot out a ship's journey and provide them with warnings and coastal markers as they navigate in the storm. Next, leaders will receive warnings about those who will defiantly try to steer the ship off course. But there will be ledges along the way that leaders must identify and learn to navigate around until or unless the Lord moves them, though the ledges appear to stand in the way of progress. The fourth chapter challenges leaders to explore their willingness to sacrifice for the ship, for its crew, and for the task the Lord has called those on the ship to fulfill. The final two chapters of the first section focus on leaders' spiritual strengths of faith in Christ and the integrity of their walk in Him. Both dimensions are sorely tested in the chaos of even the most mundane day at sea.

The second part shifts the camera angle from the helmsman's inner seascape to the skills needed to lead and train the crew. Chapter 7 discusses the importance of developing specific plans to mentor faculty members during everyday activities and in spite of overwhelming distractions. Equally important in a school's everyday process is the effective management of the change process. Chapter 9 deals with the inevitable organizational situation in which a crew member must undergo dismissal, and we will examine techniques that reflect awareness of biblical and legal standards. Also, tense situations arise in which the helmsman must be prepared to deal with conflict directly and courageously. Finally, chapter 10 examines the most pressing problem in Christian education today—the relationship between the administrator and the school board.

I believe that you can already tell from the topics mentioned in this introduction that becoming an effective helmsman is not for a weekend boater or a fair-weather sailor or the faint of heart. It requires complete dependence on the Lord as leaders dedicate themselves to personal preparation for the journey and to professional development necessary to lead the crew, who will ultimately determine the ship's arrival at its destination.

The Mindscape of the Helmsman
Qualities of a Leader's Inner World

Identifying the Lighthouses
Planning the Voyage

The ten decisions the leader must make before the storm

+ A history of lighthouses
+ Ten specific and instructive lighthouses

Numerous writers researching the origins of leadership and administration have embraced the notion that Paul's selection of the Greek word *kybernesis* to express the gift of administration in 1 Corinthians 12:28 is more than just a casual selection of a word to describe organizational skills. When we take into consideration the contemporary use during Paul's time of another form of that word, *kybernetes*—which meant *helmsman*—we view the biblical concept as communicating a powerful metaphor that includes insight, bravery, and skills to guide a ministry in the midst of a storm (Kittel and Friedrich 1985, 486; Gangel 1997, 103; Sweet 1999, 19; Coley 2006, 12). This image of a leader standing at the helm of his or her organization, diligently scanning the horizon for information about the journey, is a compelling one that should add energy and authenticity to a leader's perspective on his or her daily activities. It would naturally follow to adopt another metaphor—the lighthouse—related to the guidance of a ship's progress toward the safe arrival at its destination.

A Brief History of Lighthouses

For centuries the beacon from a lighthouse, visible for many miles to a ship at sea on a clear night, has served two primary purposes for mariners: to warn the helmsman of dangers that await his ship and crew should they come near and to guide him to a nearby harbor for safe anchorage. When visible in daylight, the unique markings on a lighthouse can serve as a landmark to give geographic bearings to sailors. At night, in our day of automation, the unique pattern of a lighthouse's beacon serves to assist a helmsman in the dark. After a brief discussion of the history of the use and value of this vital resource for a ship's leadership, I will employ this metaphor to express the importance of establishing lighthouses in our ministries. These lighthouses will offer certain assistance in the journey when consulted, certain disaster when ignored.

One of the earliest and perhaps most famous lighthouses in history is the Pharos lighthouse that stood for centuries at the mouth of the Nile River and guided Mediterranean ships into the harbor at Alexandria. Known as one of the Seven Wonders of the Ancient World, the lighthouse towered 450 feet high, and its nightly fire could be seen up to thirty miles from shore. Built in about 280 BC, the Pharos Light was built on an island just off the coast in order that helmsmen could identify the entrance to the port since the city was built on the flat Nile Delta and lacked hills or distinguishing characteristics to assist mariners miles away. To signal ships at sea, the keepers used metallic mirrors to reflect the sun by day and used the fire's blaze by night. One author describes the magnificent structure in this way:

> Ancient peoples had long made a practice of banking fires on hills and mountainsides to bring their sailors home from the sea. With its artificial mountain, Alexandria pulled in seamen from the entire known world. The delta city became the busiest and most prosperous port in the world, and it remained so for almost 1,000 years. Trading ships from Greece, Carthage, and Rome flocked to the city's wharves to load up with the grain grown in wondrous abundance in fields along the banks of the Nile. The sight of the Pharos Light burning far up near the dome of the sky must have filled the breasts of countless sea captains with awe. (Jones 1995, ix)

Having established the metaphor of an administrator as helmsman, I want to paint in your mind's eye the concept of lighthouses, which can serve as powerful companion images if we view them as symbols of significant values or decisions that provide guidance and direction to the head of school daily and to the board when it comes time to establish new policy. The following explanation can help guide the metaphor: "The purpose of a lighthouse's light is to provide a mariner at sea with a fixed point of reference to aid his ability to navigate in the dark when the shore or an offshore hazard cannot be seen directly. The distance at which such a light can be seen depends on the height and intensity of the light. The brighter the light and the greater its height above the sea, the farther it can be seen. Of course, when the weather is bad—with rain, snow, or fog—visibility can be greatly reduced" (Behring Center).

TEN LIGHTHOUSES THAT GUIDE AND WARN

The following discussion is designed to assist you in charting your course before you get caught at sea and lose your way. Are you ready to lead through a storm, to navigate it? Perhaps these ten lighthouses will help you on your way.

Lighthouse One
With whom in the evangelical community will you partner? What may seem like an unnecessary step or even an obvious point may be quickly overlooked

in an effort to "get started." Such a decision could lead to disaster through misunderstanding and the dashing of false hopes. Many schools have decided to begin with the adoption of the ACSI Statement of Faith, which provides a clearly worded document that a school can even incorporate into its handbooks and legal documents. From there the board, administration, and curriculum designers can make subsequent decisions that are of monumental importance in the everyday affairs of the school. For instance, will we endorse or require a specific version of the Bible? Which Bible curriculum will we purchase to use as our primary resource in our classes? Does that curriculum contain doctrinal statements or teaching that may be counter to our statement of faith?

The school's interactions with faculty, parents, and children, as well as with other religious leaders in the community, will affect other decisions. What do we hope to accomplish in chapel? Whom will we invite to speak? What worship styles will we encourage, accept, or deem inappropriate? Certainly the decisions about music for chapel and choir will need support from the school community.

Another dimension of the influence of this decision is the recruitment and hiring of teachers. Unless an applicant grew up in the community and attended one of the local churches, chances are that there will be a need to talk through the primary doctrinal positions of the school. Related to this discussion is the teacher's willingness to be sensitive to students who have been taught to view some aspects of worship and discipleship differently. In addition, the administration needs to assume an important role in coaching faculty members to respond appropriately when controversial issues and questions arise. At our school in Maryland, we had several Roman Catholic families who selected our school rather than local Catholic schools. Right away there was the need to express, "These are the things that we hold dear and will faithfully teach to your children."

Lighthouse Two
Will you partner with unchurched families? This question is at the heart of the question about your school's definition of *community*. Different schools have answered this question in different ways and have proved effective in reaching the students who are their target audience. My experience, along with the results of research done with the schools that are members of the Southern Baptist Association of Christian Schools, is that the majority of Southern Baptist schools

enroll students from families who are unchurched (Coley 1998, 11). Those schools believe that this approach is consistent with their sponsoring churches' commitment to evangelism and with the value of having that commitment at the core of all church ministries. However, there are many schools that have determined to enroll only children from families that have one or both parents who are committed to Christ and who attend church regularly. I am also familiar with schools that have more narrowly defined as their community those families who are active members in a specific church. Children from families who do not worship at that church may not attend that particular school.

Once again, this decision must be established in the rudiments of the school's everyday practices. Who will receive the opportunity to interview? Where will public announcements about enrollment be made, and how will they be worded? Will the application process involve the need for one or more family members to give a testimony about a personal relationship with Christ? Will the application and acceptance procedure involve requesting or requiring a reference from a pastor or a church staff member?

I think that it is important to point out that requiring students to express a personal testimony is a standard that school leaders must consider carefully. Certainly this would not be the expectation for five-year-olds entering kindergarten. Having said that, at what point is it appropriate to assume that a child or an adolescent has "had enough opportunities" and is thus no longer welcome at school? That's a call I would not want to make.

Lighthouse Three
Will you accept a student who has past discipline problems? This lighthouse naturally follows the previous question since it is somewhat related. As an experienced leader, I have found almost universal support in areas all over the United States to the following policy statement: "We do not accept a student who has been suspended or expelled from another school." Simple. Straightforward. Unambiguous. Most agree that such a statement will prevent an unsuspecting and well-meaning interviewer from making a big mistake. To do otherwise is to threaten the reputation of the ministry in the community that you are called to serve. If the Holy Spirit is leading you to help a student who has a troubled past and who wants to start fresh, then develop a restoration process that will

provide the family with a set of guidelines allowing the student to apply in the future, after a period during which he or she has established a willingness to make necessary changes and undergo a period of discipleship and accountability.

But what about students who have not been expelled but who have a reputation for being disrespectful or unruly? Once again your leadership should return to the foundational motivations and values that define what the Lord has called you to do with the specific community He has called you to serve.

Here are some metersticks, or standards of measure, that may help you decide these issues generally and decide about individual applicants specifically:

+ Are the difficulties age related, or are they signs of deeper problems that your staff may not be prepared to deal with?
+ How well prepared are the grade-level teachers to mentor and supervise a student who has that particular set of concerns?
+ What is the chemistry of the current group of students with whom that applicant will be placed? Are there strong, positive peer leadership and cooperation? Or would this applicant represent the "tipping point" for the classroom environment?
+ Do you have resources beyond the normal discipleship provided by the classroom teachers to assist in mentoring the new student?
+ Do the parents appear supportive of your school's standards? What is their appraisal of their child's past troubles?

Lighthouse Four
How much emphasis will you place on athletics? You may view this lighthouse as one you will not encounter until much later in your journey. Also, since athletics is viewed as an essential part of doing school in the minds of so many, particularly by successful leaders who gained their first experiences in leadership because they had received accolades for performances on playgrounds, some might find it puzzling that I even raise the question. Some may phrase the question this way: How can you have too much of a good thing? Developing a strong athletic program will most certainly provide many young men and women with a special place to invest God-given abilities as well as a place to expend adolescent energies. If athletics are properly organized and led, there is a never-ending source of meaningful moments from which young athletes can grow.

Unfortunately, like just about everything in life, athletics, if not properly focused and appropriately balanced, can become all-consuming to the detriment of players, fans, faculty, and the school community at large. Such dangers include allowing practice schedules and the number of games to take priority over other school, church, and family activities. Practices that seemingly never end leave the players and parents exhausted, without time for family activities or studies. Although a reasonable number of out-of-town competitions provide teams and coaches with some very special occasions to remember, repeated long-range travel can result in worn-out participants, especially bus drivers and coaches who have to teach the next day.

School leaders need to identify other rocky coastlines. Just how much attention will the "heroes" receive? Yes, students who exert great effort for a school team deserve recognition, and their success usually raises school spirit. However, those who will never participate in any form of athletic endeavor should not be made to feel that success in fine arts, ministry, or a specific area of academics is a less-important accomplishment. Second, it is crucial to avoid establishing a culture that says winning on the scoreboard and in the standings is all that matters.

I believe that it is time well spent when the community at large, the administration, the faculty, and the coaches invest in careful reflection about the emphasis on winning, the behavior of the participants and fans, and the school's reputation in regard to athletic competition. I would suggest that coaches discuss specific ways to help players grow as disciples of Christ. In addition, I strongly recommend creating teams from which there are no cuts, such as cross-country, track and field, or football, provided there are reasonable safety precautions. Using another popular approach, a school can create a second or third team at the middle-school level to avoid cutting so many young athletes who are still developing and hoping to compete. But in all things, we must constantly ask ourselves, "Does this glorify Christ, or are we bringing attention to human beings?"

In the midst of far too many negative stories about college athletes and their often-misguided coaches, George Vecsey's article "CWU Softball Players Show Compassion Beyond Sportsmanship" (*Seattle Times*, April 30, 2008) tells an inspiring story of incredible sportsmanship. Sara Tucholsky, a senior playing for Western Oregon, came to bat while two teammates were on base. For the first time in her life, Sara hit a home run over the outfield fence. As she watched the ball sail out of the park, Sara realized that during her celebration she missed first base and turned to retrace her steps. As she did so, her right knee buckled, and she lay in pain on the base path. All those involved were well aware of several rules that come into play in this situation. She had to touch all the bases to receive credit for the home run and for the run to count for her team. If a substitute runner was placed in the game, Sara's only career home run would be scored as a single. At no time could Sara receive assistance from a teammate or a coach, or she would be called out, losing the opportunity for her team to knock in another run.

But what occurred next is not covered in any rule book. Mallory Holtman, the first-base player from the opposing team, Central Washington, asked, "Excuse me, would it be OK if we carried her around and she touched each bag?" After receiving permission, two defensive players from Central Washington, Mallory Holtman and shortstop Liz Wallace, carried Sara around the diamond, pausing at each base to allow Sara to touch the base with her left foot. When Mallory was asked about her generosity and sportsmanship, she replied, "She hit it over the fence.... She deserved it. Anybody would have done it. I just beat them to it." Central Washington was knocked out of the tournament by a score of four to two, and Western Oregon continued on as Sara was scheduled for surgery. But that day, both teams were victorious.

Lighthouse Five

Will you hire a teacher who is strong academically but weak biblically? No less seductive than the worldly attraction to succeed at athletics is the temptation to be perceived as exceptionally bright or outstanding in an academic field. The siren song of academic superiority can drown out a school's original commitments to disciple young people for Christ and to model a Christlike lifestyle before students in every class period. Luke 6:40 states, "A student is not above his teacher, but everyone who is fully trained will be like his teacher" (NIV). Could Scripture be clearer? Hiring Christian role models is the most important function an administrator possesses to ensure that biblical concepts are integrated into the warp and woof of the school's curriculum and instruction. It is widely known that every one of the Ivy League schools began with a serious and passionate commitment to spread the gospel, and some even had specific objectives related to these commitments. But without exception, it took only a generation or two, and less time in some cases, for the consciousness of the school's culture to forget those biblical intentions. One of the ways that integration of biblical concepts can take place is through your school's hiring practices.

Every experienced administrator knows the trauma of losing a valued teacher only weeks or even days before school starts. I have interviewed groups of administrators on this topic, and they all agree that the Lord will provide a suitable replacement in His time. Consider this situation a test, and resolve not to be drawn into the rocks and sandbars when you face the pressure of hiring a professional teacher who has a weak or nonexistent Christian testimony.

Lighthouse Six
Will you admit students who have marginal test scores or learning uniquenesses? On the basis of my considerable experience in this area, I maintain that to admit students of all types without special planning and regard for their unique difficulties is to invite disaster. On the other hand, to steer as far away as possible from any family in distress because of a child who has learning challenges is no better than being a helmsman who ignores the SOS of a nearby vessel. The commitment of our school was to ask the Lord to show us how we could constantly expand the spectrum of special-needs students in our student body. I would hold out my hands about 5 feet apart and say to my faculty, "How can we improve our program so that more students on the academic continuum, both high achieving and low achieving, feel comfortable and accepted at our school while receiving the education that each one needs?"

As your community, your board, and your faculty wrestle with this question, there are several guidelines to consider. First, what types of learning uniquenesses are our faculty generally and certain teachers specifically qualified to address? Second, do we have a method to identify the child's weaknesses and a process to develop an appropriate course of study?* Third, does the school have necessary resources such as a designated place for therapy or tutoring as well as the means to purchase the required materials? Fourth and perhaps the most important, will the faculty and the student body share in the creation of a culture that is loving and nurturing for students who will need accommodations in mainstream classes? To be unable to answer any one of these questions with

---

*Many professionals suggest that the *Wechsler Intelligence Scale for Children* be administered by someone who is specially trained to administer and score the test.

a strong positive response is to risk defrauding a child and a family of valuable time and money. It is not enough to provide a safe, accepting environment. You must be prepared to help each child mature academically. Even so, many schools would agree that there is no greater blessing in the life of a school than to watch students who have learning difficulties succeed.

Lighthouse Seven
Will you hire a teacher who has been divorced? No one in the evangelical community needs to see any statistics on the frequency of divorce in church life today, nor does even the most casual observer or infrequent attendee of a local church need to be coached on how divisive this issue can be. It is mandatory that each administrator and his or her board wrestle with how the Lord wants them to respond to this issue before they get caught in the storm of decision making. Having hammered out a decision in advance will allow a leader to respond to the situation on the basis of a well-developed policy that is covered in prayer and researched thoroughly, free from the emotions of the moment.

When considering crucial issues such as this, the board needs to return to the school's statement of faith and the subsequent lighthouses of evangelical partnership. If those do not direct the group to a clear answer, the experienced spiritual leaders on the board or in the larger community should search the Scriptures and pray. Once the board has reached a decision, the appropriate documents should clearly state this policy, and the policy should find its way into the recruitment process and the teacher application.

With great humility and more than a little trepidation, I will state my position on this topic. The significant issues include obeying God's Word, living and sharing forgiveness with others as we ourselves have been forgiven, and providing the best role models for our children in the classroom and throughout the school. On the basis of my study of Scripture and my thirty-plus years of experience in ministry, I believe that having a divorce in one's past should not, in and of itself, eliminate someone from serving.

Lighthouse Eight
Do you desire to seek out racial diversity beyond your nondiscrimination policy? It is well-known that if your school is going to be incorporated and receive a

501(c)(3) number, then the school must publicize in some periodical in the community, such as a newspaper or a local magazine, that the school does not discriminate on the basis of race. This is a federal requirement for the school to be considered tax-exempt. Though your school can be covered under the tax-exempt status of a sponsoring church, it is still necessary to make this statement for your student body and faculty. (A related issue, but not germane for this discussion, is the future challenges that Christian ministries will face as "sexual orientation" is shoved into government standards about discrimination.)

Once again, the previous emphasis on the school board's discernment regarding the definition of *community* is crucial here. If a particular school has determined that it is a discipleship school and thus that it accepts only students from churches of like faith and worship, then a recruitment strategy to recruit students who are not members of participating churches would be counter to the school's mission. The school must ask a serious question: Are there minority students or students from families of certain socioeconomic strata who *meet our school's qualifications* but need some form of encouragement to make application? Jesus stated, "See that you do not despise one of these little ones, for I say to you that their angels in heaven continually see the face of My Father who is in heaven. For the Son of Man has come to save that which was lost" (Matthew 18:10–11).

A related consideration in this discussion is the readiness of the faculty and the student body for whatever degree of change may occur. Do both groups have leaders ready to take the lead in persuading the existing students to welcome the new ones? Do the faculty and the student body both have mature leaders who cannot be intimidated when the inevitable conflicts come from protecting the distinctives of the school? My experience says that all involved need to thoroughly pray through such change. Also, the leader of the school constantly needs to have his or her finger on the pulse of the school to anticipate conflicts before they occur.

Lighthouse Nine
How will student dress—that is, uniforms or dress-code standards—reflect your values and community culture? Few dimensions of a school's culture and its everyday comings and goings receive as much attention as its dress code. Every

school, much like every household considering the dress of the children and the parents, must go through the growing pains of deciding how the dress of its students and faculty can reflect what it stands for. And as is the case in most families, often the details of how this decision works out in everyday life changes over time. Within the past decade, my son attended a conservative Christian university for two years and received correction and even punishment for violations of minor dress-code standards that later changed while he was still attending, and the university erased even more standards without explanation during subsequent years. Here are some basic concepts that are recurring in most discussions on the topic:

• We desire to please the Lord in our dress, especially regarding modesty.
• We desire to establish an environment that is businesslike and that encourages the best mind-set for our students.
• We desire to maintain a safe, orderly environment, and a uniform manner of dress that quickly allows us to identify our students.
• We desire to require a standard of dress that is affordable.
• We desire to allow our students some range of creativity, which allows for individual preferences and needs, especially regarding each student's unique build.

I recently met the leader of an established Christian school in a western state. As the group we were a part of discussed this aspect of administration and leadership, he explained that he spent many Sundays visiting a number of area churches where students from the Christian school attended. He quickly noticed that at no church did the adults dress up and at few, if any, did women wear dresses or men wear coats and ties. Soon thereafter the new principal pointed out to his board that the school's chapel dress requirements had absolutely no meaning in the larger community, and he requested that the board drop the requirements for dresses and for dress shirts and ties. The board agreed. I think this case illustrates the importance of setting dress-code standards that represent genuine and meaningful values as opposed to setting standards that represent outdated or artificial mores.

Lighthouse Ten

Will ACSI accreditation and regional accreditation play a role in the development of your program? Having been an active participant in creating a number of Christian schools over the last few years, I can state that one of the most frequently asked, if not the number one, question is, Will this school be accredited? My experience based on conversations with hundreds of people is that nearly all of them know the importance of accreditation but that very few have a clue about what they just asked. (Lest you find me a snob, may I point out that I asked the electrician about the electrical permit for my house even though I have absolutely no idea what that involves!) No matter the age of the school, few decisions are as important as this one. The commitment to pursue initial accreditation and then the will to do what is necessary to maintain it provide the school with a lighthouse of protection and guidance that is virtually unending. Accreditation examines the school's philosophy and curriculum, its governance, its finances, its personnel procedures, and a host of other areas that are crucial to the successful and effective maintenance of the school. The best approach is to contact the ACSI office in your region and ask for information on how to get started.

Perhaps you can include in this discussion additional lighthouses that have provided you with guidance and direction in your journey as you have led your ministry. Once again, I believe that at the highest levels of leadership there is a call for vital decisions that will make all the difference in the success or failure of your institution, and I believe that to neglect these decisions is to invite disaster.

A ship's captain, fighting desperately to keep his vessel afloat amid a turbulent storm near the Lorraine Harbor at Cleveland and seeing the light from the lighthouse, asked his helmsman, "Are you sure this is Cleveland?" "Quite sure, Sir," came the response from the pilot. "But where are the lower lights?" inquired the captain. "They're out, Sir." The captain then asked, "Can you make it?" To that the helmsman replied, "We must or we'll perish, Sir!" The ship missed the channel and crashed into the rocks. Many lost their lives (Smith 1985, 182).

Earlier that evening in 1869, the keeper of the lower lights that directed ships into a safe harbor located along Lake Erie's dangerous coastline had decided he would take the night off from his arduous duties of refilling the lamps. He reasoned that after several years of his nightly duties no ships had really needed any assistance from the lower lights along the harbor. As he slept, an unexpected storm buffeted the coast, and several ships ran aground on the rocks, costing many people their lives. One man's neglect led to disaster for many even when they were so close to safety (Smith 1985, 183).

How about the board and the leadership team at your school? Is anyone who is leading your school neglecting the lighthouses that may lead your school community safely through the storm?

Recognizing the Wreckers
Identifying False Fires That Lead to Destruction

The imposters the leader must recognize in the storm

+ The definition of *wreckers*

+ Zerubbabel and his detractors

+ A model for avoiding veering off course

+ False fires in a Christian school community

+ Avoiding the drift away from scriptural moorings

While researching lighthouses and reading a marvelous book written by Ray Jones entitled *Southern Lighthouses: Chesapeake Bay to the Gulf of Mexico*, I was taken aback when I read the following description of a little town on the coast of North Carolina that is considered a favorite vacation spot of countless beachgoers every summer:

> North of Hatteras is Jockey's Ridge, a huge sand dune looking down on the town of Nags Head. The unusual names of the town and the big dune are reminders that not all guiding lights are trustworthy. It is said that the infamous "Blackbeard" and other pirates tied lanterns to the necks of horses and walked the animals along the crest of the ridge. To sailors at sea, the lanterns seemed to bob up and down like cabin lights on a ship riding the waves. This evil trick lured many unsuspecting captains too close to the shore, where their ships were trapped in the shallows and became easy prey for the pirates. Unfortunately, treachery of this kind has been common throughout history. (1995, xiii)

DEFINING WRECKERS

This account of the origin of the name Nags Head was a startling find—a remarkable legend of skulduggery about this sleepy little resort town. I had to investigate further, so I located yet another marvelous text about the history of the coastal area of my home state, *Fire on the Beach: Recovering the Lost Story of Richard Etheridge and the Pea Island Lifesavers** by David Wright and David Zoby. These two history professors include the following description of a subculture called "wreckers" (while telling about the heroic contributions of the only lifesaving station on the East Coast manned completely by black men): "Although industrious and self-sustaining, Bankers were also reputedly unruly and ungovernable. Folklore casts an infamous picture of these coastal inhabitants using various means to trick captains into beaching their ships. Many claim that the name Nags Head originated in an era when malicious wreckers would tie a lantern around an old horse's neck and lead it up and down the dunes. From the sea, the rising and falling light would give the impression of a ship safely moored in a harbor, taunting unsuspecting ship captains to sail to their destruction" (2000, 23).

I was stunned to discover that only a century and a half ago entire communities of inhabitants lured helpless strangers to financial ruin and certain death. I read on:

---

*This book, which is a must-read for Black History Month, would make an excellent addition to any school library's nonfiction section.

In these coastal communities, the cry "Ship ashore!" was followed by a frenzy of salvaging activities. Wrecking was a tradition woven into the culture from its earliest days. "Your loss, our gain" might best describe the local attitude. In the villages along the Sand Banks and on Roanoke Island, "progging"—walking about after a storm in search of valuables—was viewed as a viable occupation. At one time, the beaches were strewn with a wreck every mile, each with its own story of disaster and doom. From the deck of a wrecked schooner, the Outer Banks must have seemed a barbarous no-man's-land. (Wright and Zoby 2000, 23)

During an 1894 visit to Nags Head and Kitty Hawk, a neighboring village, American poet Robert Frost heard some of the legends of the wreckers and included in his poem *Kitty Hawk* a stanza that makes reference to the popular belief that the daughter of Aaron Burr, the man made famous by his duel with Alexander Hamilton, was tragically murdered just off the coast of North Carolina:

Did I recollect
how the wreckers wrecked
Theodosia Burr off this very shore?
'Twas to punish her
but her father more.

HELMSMAN'S LOG

The Wreckers, written by accomplished journalist and researcher Bella Bathurst, presents numerous accounts of deception, robbery, and even murder by communities throughout the British Isles: "From all around Britain I started finding stories of people deliberately drowning shipwreck victims…. There were stories of grand pianos sitting unplayed in hovels, of crofts fitted with silver candelabra, and—more recently—of an entire island dressed in suspiciously identical shirts. There were stories of false lights and false foghorns, false harbours, false rescuers, false dawns; even stories of entire coastlines rigged meticulously as stage sets" (2005, xv). ⚓

LEARNING FROM ZERUBBABEL

Should I have been surprised? From Satan's deception of Eve and then Adam in the Garden of Eden, there have been those who deceive, those who are deceived, and the wreckage that is left in the wake of the choices that people make. The Word of God provides numerous examples of temptations His people faced to change their plans, and often they did. However, in the book of Ezra, today's school leaders have an inspiring example of a leader who was undeterred in his steadfastness to stay the course that the Lord laid out for him.

The Lord moved in the heart of the pagan king of Persia, King Cyrus, and a proclamation was made that the Jews would be allowed to return home from exile in the territory formerly under the rule of their conquerors, the Babylonians. Now that Cyrus ruled in the Persian Empire, he declared that the Jews should return home and repopulate Jerusalem and rebuild the house of the Lord. More than 50,000 accepted the invitation to travel with several leaders, among them, Zerubbabel. Ezra 3:1 gives a thrilling account of unity of purpose: "The people gathered together as one man to Jerusalem." Every school leader should be so blessed! Before I introduce the bad guys, it is instructive to note that this makeshift construction crew set to work and progressed apparently unhindered until the temple's foundation was laid. Verse 11 tells of their celebration: "They sang, praising and giving thanks to the Lord, saying, 'For He is good, for His lovingkindness is upon Israel forever.' And all the people shouted with a great shout when they praised the Lord because the foundation of the house of the Lord was laid."

Enter the wreckers, stage left: "Now when the enemies of Judah and Benjamin heard that the people of the exile were building a temple to the Lord God of Israel, they approached Zerubbabel and the heads of fathers' households, and said to them, 'Let us build with you, for we, like you, seek your God; and we have been sacrificing to Him since the days of Esarhaddon king of Assyria, who brought us up here'" (Ezra 4:1–2).

A brief explanation will help identify the characters in this drama. These enemies who tried to pass themselves off as volunteers for the temple project were probably part of the tribes imported by the Assyrians to inhabit the territory left vacant by the citizens of Israel when God disciplined His children by allowing them to be conquered and taken into captivity (see 2 Kings 17:24–41). According to Jeremiah 41:5, some men from the north had in fact continued to sacrifice during the period of the exile (Williamson 1985, 49). Whether or not Zerubbabel was aware of this history is uncertain, but his extraordinary discernment and courage in his response to the enemies' offer is without question: "But Zerubbabel and Jeshua and the rest of the heads of fathers' households of Israel said to them, 'You have nothing in common with us in building a house to our God; but we ourselves will together build to the Lord God of Israel, as King Cyrus, the king of Persia has commanded us'" (Ezra 4:3).

But these wreckers of God's plan did not go away quietly! They had more false fires to set along nearby shores. First, verse 4 states that they discouraged the people of Judah. A descriptive alternate translation of the Hebrew here is "weakened the hands of" (KJV). It's tough to come up with a more precise way to describe how a faculty or an administration struggles to complete its daily tasks when it is undergoing attacks by forces operating against its mission. Second, the enemies "frightened them from building" (4:4). Though the Bible does not explain the specific techniques employed here, one can read on in this exciting book to discover political intrigue as well as threats of violence. Third, in verse 5 the reader learns that the enemies stooped to hiring "counselors" against the people of Judah to frustrate their plans. I believe these were spiritual counselors or prophets who attempted to distract the workers emotionally and spiritually. Fourth, a plot to turn the king of the empire against the new inhabitants was devised and carried out.

As you read this narrative about the detractors of God's people as the Old Testament era nears its end, does your mind jump to wreckers in your community who seek to join in so that your school will be slowly pulled off course? Does your heart rate accelerate when you think of those who discourage and counsel in the parking lot or at ball games? And there are certainly those who will launch an assault on your ministry and do their best to bait you into a public brawl. Following some navigational coaching, we will return to this discussion and attempt to identify who is behind some of the false fires and deception that Christian school leaders can encounter. Will you be prepared to identify the imposters as quickly as Zerubbabel did?

HELMSMAN'S LOG

Read the following letter that a school leader received. Identify qualities of the school's community that have helped bring about the school's contribution to the recent graduate and his family.

Dear Head of School:

As my youngest child is about to graduate from high school, I find myself often reflecting on how thankful I am that my children were given the *privilege* of attending your school.

Thanks largely to a strong biblical foundation provided by the school, my children have been solidly prepared spiritually and academically with the confidence and knowledge necessary to face life's future challenges.

These past two years have been especially difficult for my children, as they have seen their parents separate. I am tremendously grateful to the faculty and staff for their prayers and support in behalf of my son.

Our son has become a solid, intelligent young man with strong godly principles, and I believe the school's environment to be largely responsible for that because of the friendships that he has developed and because the teachers and faculty nurture and care for the whole child and not just a child's academic growth.

I would like to thank you for the impact that you have had on our son. It is obvious that you truly care about him as you have reached out to him with encouragement and direction. He often tells me about encouraging things that you have said and done for

Helmsman's Log

him, and I have been tremendously grateful to the Lord that He has had you there for my son.

This has also been an emotionally wrenching time for me, as well as for my children. Going through family hardships, I believe, is far more difficult for Christians because when your whole world revolves around the church and then you go through a divorce, often people that don't understand what has happened will react harshly toward one or both parties. When this happens to me, rather than encouraging myself to work through everything, I instead find myself withdrawing from situations that expose me to that potential.

You have been a true example to me of someone who not only says he is a Christian, but also lives the life of a Christian.

I have had my stomach in knots at some school functions and have then seen a smile or heard a word of encouragement from you that has totally brightened my outlook and made me all the more thankful for the love of God and His love and care for my children.

Anyway, I just wanted to share these thoughts with you and encourage you in your good work. You have had and continue to have a tremendous impact on the children and parents of our school, and we are very blessed to have you there. I will always be thankful for the impact that you have had on my family.

Sincerely,
The mother of a recent graduate ⚓

STAYING ON COURSE

How is it possible to stay on course while traveling in unfamiliar waters and navigating a seascape for which there is no fixed road map and to make progress toward your destination when winds and currents are constantly changing, sometimes to help you on your way and sometimes in direct opposition to your progress? As you examine the diagram in figure 2.1, consider carefully both its applications to your ministry and the ramifications of not being prepared for the false fires that have been set to pull you off course.

Mission

⇓

Vision

⇓

Excellence ⇒ **Community** ⇐ **Outcomes**

⇓

Fig. 2.1   **Governance — Curriculum — Finances**

As figure 2.1 illustrates, the foundational statement for your school is its mission statement, which informs those new to the community and reminds those associated with the school *who you are, what you do,* and *whom you serve.* The mission is tied to that community and its needs, but the mission is not bound by a specific campus or geographic location. I like to describe the perspective from the mission statement as being that of a passenger in a jet flying at 30,000 feet. From that vantage point one can form a general notion of what's below and what's coming, but it is difficult to identify specifics. Continuing the metaphor of flying, let's suppose that the passenger is now in a blimp like those that hover over a football stadium on Saturday afternoon. Now the passenger can sense the vision statement of the school. The vision statement puts feet on the mission. According to George Barna, vision is "foresight with insight based on hindsight" (1992, 28). At this point the leader is prepared to look ahead with wisdom while being aware of the realities of the present and knowledgeable about the influences of the past. Michelle Lundgren, a faculty member in the teacher education department of Grace University in Omaha, Nebraska, makes these points about the impact of a school's mission statement (2007–2008, 10):

‣ "The mission shapes a school's core identity.… Every aspect in the life of the school will reflect the very core principles of the mission statement."

+ "Since the school building itself is only a shell and since it is the people within who determine the school's destiny, the mission statement, ideally, should be in place before the hiring of school personnel. At the very least, all new personnel should be hired in light of the mission statement."

+ "The teaching that goes on in our classrooms should also be scrutinized in light of the school's mission statement.... If biblical integration and excellent classroom teaching are goals, the school leaders must identify the practical steps needed to achieve those goals."

Janet Lowrie Nason, former chair of graduate education programs at Philadelphia Biblical University, points out that every school must understand its "quiddity," or what makes it unique or different. She emphasizes that "discerning and articulating the uniqueness of a Christian school is important for everyone connected to the institution. It defines the mission and brings cohesion to parents, teachers, and students. Integrity of purpose stands at the heart of institutional identity and permeates every facet of the school's life" (2002, 3–4).

"How important is this statement of mission to the classroom, to the instruction in reading, writing, and arithmetic?" asks author and former principal Richard A. Riesen. He pointedly states, "The answer is that either it governs there or it is of no use at all.... The point of the mission statement is to inform teaching, to give it focus and emphasis." He further writes, "But to the extent that a teacher's lack of interest in the school's philosophy, at whatever level, means a failure to abide by it or advance it, to that extent there is dysfunction, or at the least a less than fully harmonious working out of the school's stated purposes." Riesen continues his adept explanation: "One of the elements of a good mission statement, therefore, in my view, is that it suggests, or at least does not obscure, the relationship between the school's larger or more philosophical aims and what is being done in its classrooms" (2006–2007, 40–41).

The next significant perspective is to define your community. This view is like that of being in a crop duster, skimming along the tops of the crops. Is your community geographically bounded? We discovered at our school in Rockville, Maryland, a suburb of Washington DC, that we had students coming from an hour's drive including students from three states and the district. Today some schools have opened their curriculum and instruction to families by using the

Internet. Is the community defined by spiritual or denominational boundaries? Will all members of the community be eligible to attend? James L. Drexler, chair of the education department at Covenant College, emphasizes the importance of community in this way: "Simply put, the notion of God's people living in relationship with one another is at the heart of the biblical teaching about the kingdom of God. The Bible regularly refers to Christians as being part of a group—the Body of Christ, the family of God, the people of God, the bride of Christ. Despite the 'rugged individualism' that is so prevalent in American culture, Christians are not a bunch of lone rangers but part of a redeemed human community" (2007–2008, 13).

Closely related to the identity of the community served by your school is your answer to the question, What is excellence? It is my experience, based on more than twenty-five years in educational administration, that this is a simple but profound topic for school leaders to discuss. Have you, your faculty, and your board ever wrestled with this question? For a moment, let's consider what the word itself means. It can mean that something in general or a specific characteristic has qualities that observers appreciate and respect. This description may seem vague or capricious, so perhaps it is better to view *excellence* from the viewpoint of a set standard that would certainly be seen as something better in a rating scale than a rating of *average* or *satisfactory*. I believe that in many people's minds the concept cannot exist apart from comparisons with other similar objects, behaviors, or activities.

So a young man could be seen as pitching an *excellent* game, on the basis of his courage, hard work, or athleticism, regardless of whether his team won. (Any parent of a player discouraged by the score may take this approach to inject some positive thoughts into a disappointing situation.) Using the second definition in the preceding paragraph, the pitcher's performance may be deemed excellent when placed on a rating scale of strikeouts, innings pitched, strikeout-to-walk-allowed ratio, or earned run averages. But what frequently happens, related to the third distinction above, is that people will place the young man's performance alongside that of the game's opposing pitcher.

A teacher's performance may be viewed as excellent because she is well liked and she meets the needs and expectations of her students and their parents from year to year. On an administrator's evaluation chart, she may be observed and evaluated on specific instructional activities. She may go beyond the stated "meets standard" and even beyond "exceeds standard" to the point of quality or frequency that is considered "excellent." Or perhaps in general when members of the school community think of her knowledge, skills, and dispositions in comparison with those of her fellow teachers, what comes to mind is, "She's an excellent teacher."

Once you and the other school leaders have considered what you mean by the term, it is time to consider what excellence looks like in your mind and in reality. Peter asks believers to consider the Lord and His *excellencies* in 1 Peter 2:9. Here the Scripture is challenging us to think about the perfections of God, though we know full well we will not attain these in our lives until we experience our glorification with Him. In this case, these characteristics are ideals that set a standard that we are supposed to consider as we live out the sanctification process.

A seasoned administrator shared with me his experience of moving to a well-established school as its new head of school. After a brief time of evaluating the school's operations and programs, he explained to me that he asked the board to remove the phrase "excellence in Christian education" from the school's letterhead until such time that the school actually delivered upon this commitment. This bold move, while startling or even humorous, helps me make my point. Upon what basis did the new leader determine that one or more qualities were *not* excellent at that point? Was it a general notion he carried in his head? Was it a lack of measurable achievements based on the school's prescribed rubric that may have come from strategic planning or accreditation recommendations? Or perhaps, and I believe the truth was behind door number three, were the achievements of his new place of service lagging behind the achievements of his previous school? My argument is this: If you do not first define *excellence*, second agree on the content or activities to be evaluated, and third determine how these will be evaluated, then the school's leaders will be vulnerable to the suggestions that they need to change course and pursue something new or exciting or fashionable. Changes may be in order, but on what basis will you make that determination?

For example, some may measure excellence in the area of athletics by conference championships, and others may measure excellence by the number of students participating in interscholastic athletics. The appearance of the facilities may be excellent in the eyes of one board member because they are clean and uncluttered, but other board members may view them as substandard when comparing them with the facilities of other schools in the neighborhood. In a rural part of the South, I recently visited a fine Christian school that meets in a building constructed in the 1930s. The building and its campus were made available to a local church when the school system determined that the citizens of the county demanded newer facilities. The church members restored all the old hardwood floors, replaced broken glass, and landscaped the grounds to restore the aging building to its original elegance. Excellent? It certainly appeared so to me as their visitor.

I discovered the importance of defining *excellence* on a Saturday afternoon while working on a particularly large, overgrown pair of shrubs in my yard. After spending an hour reducing one of these 12-foot evergreen plants to a shapely 5-foot shrub, I took a long look at my artistry and saw what I believed to be a cultured structure worthy of the British topiary found at the historic Hampton Court Palace or the famous botanical gardens located near London at Kew Gardens. After meticulously shaping one plant and removing all the clippings to the curb, I called to my wife for her evaluation before attacking the plant's mate standing next to it. Though I was confident she would admire my work and declare the new look excellent, she quickly and decisively declared that the monster was still much too large and that she would be happier if it were removed altogether! (She prefers delicate, low-growing azaleas!) Unfortunately for the part-time gardener, she deemed the laborer's work anything but excellent.

Isn't this the case in all-too-many board meetings, when an energetic administrator rolls out a heartfelt presentation that took weeks to develop, only to be met with reluctance and skepticism? In his mind are the first steps to a new level of achievement for the school. In the minds of one or more board members are the beliefs that less is more, that the school is acceptable the way it is, and that change always requires more money, a requirement that translates into higher tuition. Perhaps in the minds of others is the matter of unfinished business that is of vital concern to them. Perhaps also the proposed changes appear as inconvenient distractions to the administrators. This scenario occurs time and time again because of the lack of agreement on the question, What does excellence look like?

HELMSMAN'S LOG

Imagine a new school in the Midwest established by a widow who made a small fortune from her family's ranch. She worked tirelessly to see that the school had the best construction materials and design available, and she spared no expense in equipping and staffing the school. When it came to selecting a head of school, she turned to a local acquaintance who had served with her in a parachurch ministry. She was confident that her friend would lead the school to achieve excellence.

The first year began with great energy and enthusiasm, though many members of the local community took a wait-and-see attitude. Because of the pressing demands of the new position, the administrator hurried some purchasing decisions that upset the school's benefactors. In an effort to put the much-needed operational procedures in place, the young leader made another unpopular decision: his administrative assistants would handle his calls and walk-in inquiries. This decision prompted more negative feedback to the school's founder. The remainder of the first year included the successful creation of numerous school activities, the acceptance of the school's ten graduates into college, and surprisingly impressive performances by the school's athletic teams. However, board meetings consisted of stressful discussions about the school's development of a budget that would not require constant transfusions of money. The outward appearance of success masked the growing disapproval of some of the board

HELMSMAN'S LOG

members who seemed to be a magnet for anyone who had any level of disagreement with the head of school.

Year two saw the school's enrollment double and the school's best teachers return. A new football coach attracted new players from other schools in the area. These new additions led to startling victories on the field and unexpected exposure in the local newspaper. These successes brought a sense of euphoria on the part of everyone but a handful of board members. The sudden jump in enrollment brought increased expenses, and the budget spiraled out of control. Although the youthful administrator garnered new friends and support out in the community, he seldom had time for phone calls and one-on-one meetings with board members. Though teachers were meeting instructional goals and the school's atmosphere was very positive, it seemed that the only reports reaching the ears of some board members were the complaints of a small number of families.

If the school called you in to consult, to what benchmarks, or lighthouses, would you direct the leadership's attention? In what ways would the administrator describe the school's performance as excellent? Would the board's view be different? ⚓

Having wrestled with the definition of your community and the complexity of your leadership's vision of excellence, you must next turn your attention to what you believe should be the outcomes of all you do at your school. To put it simply, ask the question, What does a graduate of our school look like when he or she shakes the hand of our administrator and receives a diploma at graduation? I would argue that many school boards have not given that question enough consideration. Bruce Lockerbie, chair of Paideia Inc., articulates a clear and compelling response to this question when he writes the following:

> An essential goal in molding disciples of Jesus Christ is to develop in them a maturing biblical worldview. No Christian school is worthy of the claim of having a biblical perspective on teaching and learning unless its philosophy of pedagogy is worldview oriented. It is not that the Christian school imposes a biblical worldview on its students, as if brainwashing were a test of discipleship. Yet worldview awareness is—for this generation—what the integration of faith and learning represented 50 years ago: a new way of speaking about the commitment to bring every thought, every concept, every theory, every hypothesis, every axiom into submission to the lordship of Jesus Christ. A biblical worldview is the philosophical end for which Abraham Kuyper's stunning declaration is the premise: "There is not a square inch in the whole domain of our human existence over which Christ, who is Sovereign over all, does not cry: 'Mine!'" (2007–2008, 7)

Returning to figure 2.1, I would like to call to your attention that all too often board members and other leaders first plan the governance of their school before considering the definition of the community that will be the focus of the mission statement. From what dimensions of the surrounding communities are your leaders selected if there is not clarity of thought and distinction preceding the design of the governance and of such documents as the articles of incorporation and the bylaws? A church-sponsored school may want to consider only its own church members eligible for participation on the school board, but it would be important to consider representation from the variety of members that make up the church. A community Christian school would need to consider the participation of pastors or leaders from like-minded area churches that the school hopes will be participating in the school's makeup.

Likewise, many school leaders jump to planning curriculum and finances before establishing the elements of community, excellence, and outcomes. When considering the development of your school's educational program, you and the other school leaders must agree that "education should address the immediate and future needs of the students" (Uecker 2007–2008, 15), but to do so without first determining to whom God is calling you to minister ends up being an exercise in the purchasing of a box of random resources from one of the many large publishing houses that are well-known to parents. I met a leader from a Hispanic community near Orlando, Florida, who started a Christian high school. He wants to see it expand to include a two-year community college that will offer trade skills. My friend Daniel has it! His plan includes a vision that is connected to a specific community and includes outcomes that dictate the curriculum for the course of study. And as his board develops its perspective of excellence, it will be able to plan and structure its design for the school's finances. All too often school decision makers begin with the question, What can our parents afford? before those decision makers have determined what they wish to accomplish and the resulting per-pupil cost to educate. Some boards I have met with freely admit that they started with the issue of making their tuition affordable and worked back from there! There has to be a better way. May I again urge you to track your planning steps through the flow of figure 2.1 from top to bottom and not from bottom to top?

IDENTIFYING FALSE FIRES

Wreckers in a Christian school community set the following false fires I have encountered:

False fire one. "I want my child to attend an Ivy League school." Because our school was located in the DC area and New England was a few hours away, this group of Ivy League colleges and universities held sway and called out to many parents as the sirens did Ulysses. What we heard the parents saying was, "We want the best possible opportunity academically, and the prestige wouldn't hurt our children either." Our immediate reaction was that our curriculum and teachers should challenge their students to be their best in all the basic college-prep subjects and many of the popular electives. However, the ambitions of the parents did not become our outcome goal. We deeply believed in Matthew 6:33: "But seek first His kingdom and His righteousness, and all these things will be added to you." And yes, the latter includes a prestigious New England school if that is where the Lord wants a student to continue to prepare for His service and perhaps meet the mate He wants him or her to marry.

False fire two. "I want my child to earn an athletic scholarship." Once again a seductive goal can lure our leaders and coaches away from a biblical approach. Focusing on the ambition of impressive victories and achievements in order to propel young athletes to the next level can ruin teamwork and relationships with fellow Christian schools, as well as present a weak or nonexistent testimony to unbelievers from other schools, be they players, coaches, officials, or spectators. Claude E. "Bud" Schindler Jr., author and longtime leader at Dayton Christian Schools, has written cogently and powerfully on this topic:

> The Christian approach to athletics must stem directly from the school's Christian philosophy of education, since it is foundational to everything done in the school system. A brief philosophical statement of athletics could be "to develop the spiritual part of the athlete so that the Holy Spirit is in control and directing his mind and body" (I Thessalonians 5:23)....
>
> ... "Our major purpose is to cause our athletes to act and think like Jesus Christ.
>
> "We want our athletes to possess positive Christ-like character qualities and to express them openly through the medium of athletics. We are most interested in building eternal values in our athletes and therefore need to stress attitudes and actions in relation to God's Word." (1987, 106–7; material within quotation marks in second and third paragraphs taken from Dayton Christian Schools' written statement of philosophy of coaching)

In their zeal to establish a winning program, many coaches have failed to consider the damage their behavior does to the school's reputation, not to mention the lost opportunity to model Christlike behavior for students and parents. North Raleigh Christian Academy (NRCA) in Raleigh, North Carolina, has established a "no comment policy" to reinforce the standard that a coach's reaction to the authority of officials must be exemplary. The policy reads, "Coaches will make no comments verbally or by gesture to a game official on judgment calls. Coaches may make inquiries of a game official, during the appropriate time, on a rule or game administrative procedure" (NRCA Administration 2009, 5).

At our school in Maryland, we were blessed by having in our student body a group of young women who liked to play fast-pitch softball, and they were very good at the game. In the midst of a championship season, a player on an opposing team that our team had just defeated by a large margin gave us a great victory worth more than any trophy: "Your team is our favorite team to play even though we lose by a lot of runs. You are great sports, you enjoy your teammates, and you encourage us while we play." And along the way four of those young women whom I had the privilege to coach played college softball. Our perspective was this: What does it profit a student if that student gains a career goal in professional sports but loses his or her soul?

False fire three. "I want my child to develop the social skills, such as social dancing, needed to succeed in college activities." A desire for students to develop such skills as social dancing is curious and controversial on a number of levels. Please consider these reservations that some believers have for not sponsoring a prom that includes dancing. The first and most obvious is the disconnect that occurs when we contemplate the countless resources that have been garnered and invested in a school community to glorify our Savior and to disciple young people. Contrast that investment with the time and resources dedicated to a function that may be construed as a worldly entanglement by some in that same school community.

Here's a simple test. If you discovered a boy and girl in a prolonged embrace in the hall, what would be your reaction—at least a sharp command to break it up or maybe a detention? Now, fast-forward to the slow dance that evening at the party sanctioned by your school. Would you not say that subsequently condoning slow dancing is confusing to the students? Some readers may disagree with the previous logic, but there's a second point to consider.

When parents enroll their children, would you agree that they make the assumption or prediction that their children will be able to attend or participate in every activity sponsored by like-minded Christians? On the other hand, would school leaders knowingly sponsor an activity that they are confident one or more students will not be allowed to attend? Do the dance sponsors, then, appear indifferent or callous to the heartbreak of kids who hustle every day to fit in with their peer groups and who are left at home on a big weekend of their senior year? Most of us would agree that this scenario is a shame and that it should be avoided, even if it means not sponsoring an activity that the majority in today's culture would not only accept, but embrace as a rite of passage.

Third, many schools invest extraordinary efforts on social dancing, apparently oblivious to the sexual temptation that besets many young people. True, this struggle takes place in many battlefields, but why would leaders parade their troops into what is likely to be an enemy stronghold for many?

False fire four. "I want my child in a competitive environment so that he or she will be pushed." Gloria Stronks and Doug Blomberg coedited the compelling book *A Vision with a Task: Christian Schooling for Responsive Discipleship,* in which they provide valuable insights into effective formation of a Christian community and conversely the presence of forces pulling against those who wish to develop such a community. In the chapter "Challenges to the Vision: Cultural Constraints in the Nineties," Stronks and Blomberg warn of the destructive nature of competition, an ingredient underlying several of the preceding subjects described as false fires. Sighting several research articles, they express deep concern that Christian school programs too often are not distinctive from those of any other school and that they are "fragmented, superficial, and deeply antithetical to Christian presuppositions and purposes." To a large extent the perceived need for competition drives these weaknesses: learning and achievement almost always take place through comparisons with others. It doesn't stop there:

> Grading, however, is not the only form of competition in the schools. This is because spelling bees, science fairs, and the state band competition are used as a form of control: "The class that sells the most magazine subscriptions will get a pizza party!" Even group efforts such as the athletic team end the year by appointing a Most Valuable Player. The system needs winners; just as important, the system needs losers. We give dignity only to those who achieve....
>
> The questions surrounding competition and the subculture of schooling go straight to the heart of schooling in general and Christian schooling in particular: *"Is there no other way to control and motivate students?"* Competition, along with other bureaucratic structures, is an institutional tool that promotes conformity rather than the unwrapping of individual gifts." (1993, 45; italics in original)

Once again, I appreciate the insights and commitments of Bud Schindler, who states that his school has tried to bring its sports program more in line with God's way of doing things. Rather than continuing the tradition of "best offensive player" or "best defensive player," the coaches have begun the practice of creating awards that are based on positive character qualities such as endurance, diligence, and cooperation (1979, 56).

Protecting Your School's Future by Training Faithful Leaders

Fulfilling your obligation to recognize wreckers and identify their false fires doesn't end with just your commission on the ship; you are supposed to train wise and faithful leaders to carry on after you depart (see chapter 7 for the development of this skill). Alas, many schools do not survive after the departure of their founders. Bruce Lockerbie tells of the founding of the Northfield Young Ladies' Seminary in 1879 and of Mount Hermon Boys' School in 1881, both by evangelist Dwight L. Moody and his supporters to prepare young people whose faith in Jesus Christ would be grounded in Scripture (2007, 312). In a sermon delivered at New York City's Fifth Avenue Presbyterian Church just six weeks before his death, Moody expressed his deep affection for these two institutions:

> Five and twenty years ago in my native village of Northfield I planted two Christian schools for the training of boys and maidens in Christian living and consecration as teachers and missionaries of Jesus Christ. I bequeath as my legacy those training schools for Jesus to the churches of America, and I only ask that visitors to the beautiful native village where my ashes slumber on consecrated Round Top when they go there shall not be pained with the sight of melancholy ruins wrought by cruel neglect, but rather shall be greeted by the spectacle of two great, glorious lighthouses of the Lord, beaming out over the land, over the continent, over the world. (Curtis 1962, 297–98)

Unfortunately, it took a matter of only a few short years to pollute Moody's dream. "Within a decade of Moody's death, Northfield Mount Hermon—as these merged schools are known today—had forsaken the orthodoxy of the founder, as Moody's successors diluted the religious persuasion of the earlier evangelical faculty" (Lockerbie 2007, 312–13).

Looking for Ledges
Distinguishing the Immovable

The realities the leader must accept until the Lord moves

+ The definition of *ledges*

+ Some examples of ledges in Christian schools

+ Old Testament leaders who looked to God regarding their ledges

Along the New England coast there exist massive rocks called ledges around which young sailors must learn to navigate. Every school administrator faces the challenge of identifying ledges, or those aspects of the school and the community that are immovable. To neglect doing so is to risk ramming into the ledges and allowing the certain destruction of the school.

Defining Ledges

Most of us think of ledges as only being offshore or freestanding in the ocean. I learned otherwise in late 2006 through an e-mail exchange with Floyd Calderwood, who taught me much about ledges from his years of living on the coast of Maine. Rocks that plunge into the sea from the land are also referred to as ledges. Some ledges are above water all the time, some are visible only at low tide, and some lurk just below the level of the water even at the lowest of the tides.

In essence, ledges can be terrifying obstacles, but they also provide shelter and habitat, break big waves, and provide guideposts. Although there is a windward side to all things, there is also a leeward side. If a helmsman can learn to navigate to the leeward side—not always the same side because of different currents and wind direction—without the consequences of grounding on a ledge, he can find the shelter and see the majesty instead of the obstacle.

Many ledges are marked by lighthouses that sit on the ledges when the ledges are visible above the water or even when the ledges themselves are below the water. This type of light is common at the entrance to harbors or where the light is offshore. Building a light on any type of ledge has never been an easy task, and erecting some lighthouses—such as Minot's Ledge off the coast of Massachusetts—has been especially difficult.

It's uncertain when an offshore rock becomes a ledge or a ledge becomes an island. One of the most famous very low-lying islands or ledges is Sable Island, a Canadian island off the coast of Nova Scotia. Since 1583 more than 350 shipwrecks have been recorded off the coast of this island, whose name is French for *sand*.

In 1989 one of the most famous shipwrecks in history occurred off the coast of Alaska—the collision of the oil tanker *Exxon Valdez* with a reef in Prince William Sound, creating the worst environmental disaster up to that time. It was estimated that eleven million gallons of crude oil spilled in the accident. More recently a Greek cruise liner, *Sea Diamond*, hit a reef off the coast of Greece. All 1,195 passengers and 391 crew members were evacuated before the 469-foot ship sank.

Although ledges have earned a much-deserved reputation as wreckers of ships, ledges also provide many benefits. Ledges, particularly reefs, which may be described as continuous ledges, provide protection to harbors and sometimes entire coastlines. In addition, they provide a habitat for many species of sea creatures, such as puffins, which are intriguing animals that live in colonies. Large ledges, known as banks or grounds—for example, the Grand Banks off the coast of Newfoundland—serve as the locations of valuable fisheries.

Ledges in Christian Schools

As a young administrator of a rapidly growing school in suburban Maryland, I faced several ledges that could not be ignored and that would not budge. At the top of the list was the noticeable absence of a gymnasium for our growing sports program. We were left to depend on the availability of rental space around the immediate area, the kindness of others more fortunate, and the understanding of the other teams in our conference. Needless to say, all games were away games, and we never had the advantage of being comfortable on a home court. We did, however, have a small cafeteria with a 15-foot ceiling, so we were able to shuttle three or four teams through on a rotating basis when other space was unavailable. Each day after lunch we folded the rolling tables and stored them away and did the best we could to sweep the floor so that physical education classes could use the space as well. And occasionally we had to strategically place a cloth or two on the floor to absorb drips from the ceiling during a heavy rain.

Fast-forward to the NBA draft of 2007. The number two player taken in the draft that year was a freshman from the University of Texas who had been named the NCAA player of the year. Kevin Durant, who would become the Rookie of the Year in the NBA, was a 2006 graduate of the school where I was in ministry. I never had the privilege of meeting him, but a close friend taught him and gave an enthusiastic account of Kevin's Christian testimony.

How did Kevin's basketball career begin in a school with no gym? After I prayed for ten years that the Lord would remove this ledge in our midst, the sponsoring-church and school communities joined hands to raise a significant amount of the total necessary to build a beautiful facility that would contain much-needed space including a full-size high-school gymnasium. I was deeply thankful for how the Lord worked in that situation, and I was also reminded that we had not despised the small things we did have that allowed us to grow a first-class program while we waited for Him to provide for our needs.

A second ledge was removed in a mysterious way. One of our three buildings, the oldest wing in the complex, was built during the 1960s when it was common practice to include asbestos in the ceiling material and in the floor tiles. Not only did the presence of asbestos cause concern when it came to cleaning and maintenance, but we also had to maintain legally required records related to the oversight of the facility. In addition, we were not allowed to make renovations of any space containing asbestos because disturbing the material makes anyone in the area at risk for breathing the harmful fibers.

One Saturday evening or Sunday morning, a complete stranger to everyone in the church and the school entered this building and set three small fires that burned quickly and would have consumed the entire wing had it not been for the presence of a custodian who had arrived early to make final preparations for Sunday worship. The fires did no structural damage, but the smoke damage required the removal of all the asbestos—floor and ceiling. In God's providence, our insurance coverage included the extremely expensive removal of all the dangerous material. What man meant for evil, God used for good (Genesis 50:20).

Our third ledge remained intact during my administration. We were landlocked and unable to grow to meet the increasing demands of the school community. Careful planning and almost perpetual renovations and construction of new space allowed the school to increase enrollment every year, but we finally hit a capacity beyond which we could not expand. As of the time I left to teach graduate studies, the school had determined no long-term solution. However, such was not the case at a good friend's school in Garner, North Carolina.

Mike Woods, a graduate of Wake Christian Academy and a former teacher and middle-school principal, now heads the school. He has watched the school develop over the years to its current population of 1,100 and has led the board to pray for the Lord's direction in responding to the ever-increasing demands of the community surrounding their forty-acre campus. When land contiguous to the school property became available in the late 1990s, the school approached local county officials about the cost of running the city sewage system the short distance necessary for the school to make a connection and use the property. The school leaders were stunned to receive the response that the cost would be entirely prohibitive for the school even to consider. However, after the passing of about eight years and apparently in God's timing, other construction plans beyond the school's property made it necessary for the authorities to run the pipes past the property and reduce the cost of connection by 80 percent!

Old Testament Leaders Who Waited on God

Are you willing to wait on the Lord's plan and design for your life, your career, and the changes you believe your ministry needs? Consider a few Old Testament people whom the Lord placed in strategic positions:

+ Abraham received a covenantal promise from the Lord: "For I have made you the father of a multitude of nations" (Genesis 17:5). But for *decades* this man and his wife were unable to have a son through whom the Lord could fulfill His promise. Finally after a long wait, the announcement came and there was laughter (Genesis 18:10–12)!
+ Isaac had to wait for Jacob because Rebekah was barren. But after Isaac prayed, the Lord responded by giving him and Rebekah twin boys (Genesis 25:21).
+ Jacob was brokenhearted over what he thought was the death of his firstborn from his wife Rachel. But twenty-two years later Jacob and Joseph would be reunited in Egypt according the Lord's plan (Genesis 45:8, 46:29–30).
+ Moses was called upon to study on the backside of the desert (Exodus 3:1, KJV) in preparation for his leadership of an entire nation (Exodus 3:10). Not until Moses was eighty years of age did God tell him to return to Egypt and thereby respond to the call of God to lead His children.

- Joshua and Caleb were right! But they were required to suffer and wait with all those of the younger generation until the unfaithful generation perished in the desert. Joshua did not waste those years by being bitter or indolent but served as the understudy of Moses in preparation for God's call. Caleb, though a man of eighty-five, was ready to lead in every way—physically, emotionally, and spiritually—when the time came to take possession of the most rugged country in the Promised Land.

- David, a shepherd boy, was anointed to be the next king of Israel and was heralded throughout the kingdom for his exploits in battle. However, he could not ascend to the throne until the Lord removed King Saul. In the meantime David and his mighty men spent time fleeing the spiteful Saul, and during that period they had to hide in dark caves (1 Samuel 22:1–5) and live in other difficult circumstances.

- Zerubbabel and those who were rebuilding the temple in Jerusalem following their return from Babylon were under constant pressure from the locals to cease their construction efforts. The temple builders were doing the will of God and attempting to bring glory to Him as they restored His house, but the political forces against them prevailed, and the work was stopped for several years until the time was right for restoration to begin again (Ezra 4:23–24).

- Nehemiah was deeply moved by the accounts of the disgraceful condition of Jerusalem and was under tremendous conviction to take action to rectify the situation. Nehemiah 1:4 gives his reaction from his perspective: "I sat down and wept and mourned for days; and I was fasting and praying before the God of heaven." Here was a leader with extraordinary motivation and exceptional patience to wait on the Lord. Nehemiah remained constant in prayer until God moved the king to inquire about Nehemiah's countenance.

Take a step back from your current situation and rethink the vision the Lord has given you. First, is it really His vision or a collection of personal dreams and ambitions? Next, consider this question: Did His vision come with microwavable instructions? I do not think so. Most leaders receive a big-picture view to share with others, and then the leaders must work patiently day by day to follow the leading of God as He directs—including avoiding collisions with those obstacles that frustrate those leaders but do not go unseen by God. In His time you will be able to recognize how and why God has used the ledges in your ministry.

Serving by Sacrifice
Setting the Example

The crucial ingredient many leaders lack in the storm

+ Two leaders who risked their lives to save victims of a shipwreck

+ Robert Greenleaf and Thomas Sergiovanni on servant leadership

+ Three Old Testament administrators who sacrificed and served

+ Jesus' model of servanthood

+ Reasons servant leadership is needed in today's culture

H ave you determined that you have the courage and the fortitude to sacrifice for those you are called to serve? Many will be caught in storms, not of your making, and will cry out for help.

SACRIFICIAL LEADERSHIP

Thomas Steinise faced a situation demanding leadership and sacrifice on August 21, 1933, when Maryland was hit by a storm so violent that it destroyed hundreds of homes and ships along the Atlantic coast and in the Chesapeake Bay. Steinise was the lighthouse keeper at Seven Foot Knoll Lighthouse and was confident that the structure could stand up to the ninety-mile-per-hour winds and fifteen-foot waves, just as it had in the past (Jones 1995, 9).

Above the roar of the wind, he heard a disturbing sound, the high-pitched signal of a vessel in distress. The distress call came from the *Point Breeze*, a tugboat that had been searching for the safety of a harbor when it was swamped by the massive waves. The struggling tug sank within 500 yards of the lighthouse (Jones 1995, 9).

Without regard for his own safety, the keeper lowered the station's twenty-one-foot rescue boat into the treacherous water and pulled with all his strength toward the wreck. For more than two hours Steinise fought the storm single-handedly in his small craft and managed to rescue six members of the drowning crew. Following this dramatic rescue, he received a congressional medal for heroism. The modest keeper told reporters, "Just doing what was right" (Jones 1995, 9).

In 1928 another act of sacrifice had taken place off the Florida coast at the Jupiter Inlet Lighthouse. A hurricane knocked out the newly installed electrical system just when the passing ships needed its guidance most. The teamwork between father and son that night saved countless lives, and it is truly inspiring: "Keeper Charles Seabrook, despite a severely infected hand, reinstalled the light's old mineral lamps but was too weakened by pain to operate them manually. Seabrook's sixteen-year-old son persuaded his father to let him climb the tower, by now an inverted pendulum swaying seventeen inches off-center. The boy proved himself a man as he turned the light by hand and kept it moving for four harrowing hours" (Jones 1995, 70).

HELMSMAN'S LOG

In 1860 the Olympian Ed Spencer was attending Northwestern University in Evanston, Illinois. During a fierce storm one evening, Spencer was studying in the library and was interrupted by the shouts of classmates who reported the certain destruction of a ship that had been caught on the rocks on nearby Lake Michigan. They informed him that many people were on board and that the chance of their rescue was bleak (Smith 1985, 177).

The young athlete ran to the coastline without a moment's hesitation and began stripping away his outer garments. The currents were still treacherous, though the storm had subsided. He fought through the rolling waves and reached the stranded vessel and returned to shore with the first passenger to be rescued. After repeating this feat several more times, it is said that friends on the shore told him, "Ed, you've done all you can. You'll surely kill yourself if you try it anymore." The Olympian's reply was simply, "I've got to do my best." He plunged back into the surf over and over again until he had carried seventeen passengers to safety. Finally, he could go no further and fell unconscious on the beach. Throughout the night while he lay in the infirmary, he repeated the same question over and over, "Have I done my best, fellows? Fellows, have I done my best?" (Smith 1985, 177).

Although those he rescued would return to their normal lives, the health of Ed Spencer was broken, and he would spend the rest

HELMSMAN'S LOG

of his life as a semi-invalid. Many years later a visitor to his home discovered the figure of a man who was a shadow of his former self. The stranger interviewed him about the heroic night and returned home to pen the hymn "Have I Done My Best for Jesus?" (Smith 1985, 177–78). ⚓

SERVANT LEADERSHIP

Though certainly not the only author to discuss "servant leadership," Robert K. Greenleaf popularized the phrase in his work over several decades. He introduces the principle this way:

> A new moral principle is emerging, which holds that the only authority deserving one's allegiance is that which is freely and knowingly granted by the led to the leader in response to, and in proportion to, the clearly evident servant stature of the leader. Those who choose to follow this principle will not casually accept the authority of existing institutions. *Rather, they will freely respond only to individuals who are chosen as leaders because they are proven and trusted as servants.* To the extent that this principle prevails in the future, the only truly viable institutions will be those that are predominantly servant led. (2002, 23–24; italics in original)

And how are we to identify such a leader? Greenleaf argues that these individuals are *servants first* and that the best test of their leadership is this: "Do those served grow as persons? Do they, *while being served*, become healthier, wiser, freer, more autonomous, more likely themselves to become servants? *And*, what is the effect on the least privileged in society? Will they benefit or at least not be further deprived?" (2002, 27; italics in original). By contrast, the *leader first* "serves out of promptings of conscience or in conformity with normative expectations" (28).

Thomas J. Sergiovanni, a widely known author on educational leadership, builds on this approach and places his concepts in the setting of an educational community by connecting the impact of this style to the establishment of the core values and purposes of the institution: "Servant leadership provides legitimacy partly because one of the responsibilities of leadership is to give a sense of direction, to establish an overarching purpose." As the leader of the school serves the members of his or her community, trust is built as the members learn that the leader is making decisions on the basis of competence and the values of the community, rather than on the basis of self-interest. Sergiovanni states, "Servant leadership is more easily provided if the leader understands that serving others is important but that the most important thing is to serve the values and ideas that help shape the school as a covenantal community. In this sense, all the members of a community share the burden of servant leadership" (1992, 124–25).

In *The Principalship*, Sergiovanni (1995, 320) points out to his readers that the basic tenets of this approach are found in the Bible, specifically in Matthew 20:25–27: "Ye know that the princes of the Gentiles exercise dominion over them, and they that are great exercise authority upon them. But it shall not be so among you: but whosoever will be great among you, let him be your minister; and whosoever will be chief among you, let him be your servant" (KJV).

Sergiovanni powerfully summarizes the preceding discussion by pulling together the concepts of values, purposes, ministering, moral authority, and service to members of your community:

Servant leadership describes well what it means to be a principal. Principals are responsible for "ministering" to the needs of the schools they serve. The needs are defined by the shared values and purposes of the school's covenant. They minister by furnishing help and being of service to parents, teachers, and students. They minister by providing leadership in a way that encourages others to be leaders in their own right. They minister by highlighting and protecting the values of the school. The principal as minister is one who is devoted to a cause, mission, or set of ideas and accepts the duty and obligation to serve this cause. Ultimately her or his success is known by the quality of the followership that emerges. Quality of followership is a barometer that indicates the extent to which moral authority has replaced bureaucratic and psychological authority. When moral authority drives leadership practice, the principal is at the same time a leader of leaders, follower of ideas, minister of values, and servant to the followership. (1995, 320)

In the popular book *Leadership by the Book: Tools to Transform Your Workplace*, authors Ken Blanchard, Bill Hybels, and Phil Hodges create a fable in which a professor, Blanchard, and a minister, Hybels, counsel an imaginary rising-star businessman, Michael. The following excerpt comes from their discussion on servant leadership:

"People with servant hearts have certain characteristics and values in common as they make leadership decisions. *Their paramount aim is the best interests of those they lead.*"

"In other words," said Michael, "personal power, recognition, or money is never the focus."

"Never," insisted the Minister. "That's why servant leaders are willing to share power. Their purpose is to equip other people to become freer, more autonomous, more capable—and therefore more effective."

"Servant leaders must get *personal satisfaction from watching the growth and development of those they lead,*" observed the Professor.

"Exactly," continued the Minister. "When you combine that attribute with having *a loving care for those they lead,* you know you're dealing with a different kind of leader."

"That's interesting. But how about accountability?" asked Michael.

"Leaders with servant hearts *want to be held accountable for their behavior and results,*" said the Minister. "They want to know whether they have been helpful to those they're serving."

"I bet that means they *are willing to listen,*" commented the Professor.

"That's a given," said the Minister. "They receive criticism and advice as a gift even when it isn't offered for positive reasons. Anything you say that will help them do a better job is welcome. After all, their aim is to serve."

"This all sounds great," said Michael, "but what keeps servant leaders from going crazy trying to please everyone?"

"I know some people think that's what servant leadership is all about— pleasing everyone," said the Professor. "That couldn't be farther from the truth. And it's one of the great principles that Jesus demonstrated."

"Jesus certainly didn't try to please everyone," said the Minister. "His single concern in his leadership was to please God. To me, true servant leaders want to serve and help people to accomplish their goals and be effective, but ultimately they're seeking to please only one—the Lord."...

... [The Minister continued,] "As a leader, we're called to serve. If we accept that calling, good results will follow. People tend to exceed expectations when they're led by someone who cares about them and has their best interests in mind. Without a relationship with the caller—God has been edged out—people tend to get prideful and start to think they deserve the credit when the results and the applause come. True servant leaders know where the credit belongs." (1999, 66–69; italics in original)

Old Testament Servant-Leaders

Have you ever considered what extraordinary administrators some of the Old Testament heroes were? Rethink the preceding discussion on servant leadership as the concepts apply to Joseph, Daniel, and Nehemiah. Do you see a pattern? All three became extremely successful, though starting from a point of servitude to foreign masters in an alien country. Each worked tirelessly for the good of others, not just for the primary master or ruler, but for all those around them. When called upon to give an account of their influence or to speak to the king, here's what each had to say:

Joseph. " 'I cannot do it,' Joseph replied to Pharaoh, 'but God will give Pharaoh the answer he desires' " (Genesis 41:16, NIV). The NASB renders the first phrase, "It is not in me."

Daniel. "No wise man, enchanter, magician or diviner can explain to the king the mystery he has asked about, but there is a God in heaven who reveals mysteries" (Daniel 2:27–28, NIV).

Nehemiah. "Then I prayed to the God of heaven, and I answered the king, 'If it pleases the king and if your servant has found favor in his sight, let him send me to the city in Judah where my fathers are buried so that I can rebuild it' " (Nehemiah 2:4–5, NIV).

The second obvious quality of these three administrators is their commitment to the fact that the Lord was their source and that He deserved all the glory! God used Joseph in a magnificent way when Joseph served as the administrator over all of Egypt. Daniel was the ruler over the entire province of Babylon and later the whole kingdom of Persia. Nehemiah became the governor of Judah during the restoration of Jerusalem. Each submitted to God's purpose in his life and served diligently where he was placed. Each humbled himself before the Lord and determined that the Lord deserved all the credit for any accomplishment.

THE ULTIMATE SERVANT-LEADER

No clearer examples of servant leadership can be found than those in the pages of the Gospels—accounts of Jesus, the ultimate servant-leader, as described by His contemporaries. On one occasion Luke takes his readers down a crowded street in a town near the Sea of Galilee. In recent days Jesus had taught and healed, contended with demons, and calmed a violent storm. The disciples must have been filled with amazement, and they must have been eager to see what miracle would occur next. They would soon find out.

The Master and His disciples were pushing their way through a congested street. To describe the crowd's proximity to Jesus, Luke uses the same Greek word—translated here as "pressing" (8:42)—that he used in Luke 8:14 to describe the work of the thorns that "choked" the good seed. During this pressing, Jesus and the disciples encountered Jairus, a prominent community member and a leader of the synagogue. Suddenly this man of prestige fell in the dust at Jesus' feet, pleading for the Teacher's healing touch, for Jairus' only daughter was near death (8:41–42). Jesus agreed to accompany the dispirited father, and the small group once more set off, moving slowly through the mass of onlookers and followers.

The crowd failed to notice a woman who is described as dealing with a debilitating medical problem of bleeding that had continued for twelve years (Luke 8:43). What did this condition mean for a woman in Jewish society during this time? Physically, the woman was no doubt severely anemic and probably weak and pale. The Gospel of Mark points out that she had seen a number of doctors and that their remedies had only made her worse! Financially, she had spent all that she had in her effort to find a cure (Mark 5:26). Socially and spiritually, her culture considered her unclean, an outcast; and it would continue to do so unless the bleeding ceased and she followed the prescribed guidelines for cleansing in the temple. Emotionally, she was drained and filled with despair. Perhaps she had not received a hug from anyone during the entire twelve years.

Powerfully and succinctly, Luke explains that the woman was instantly healed after touching the cloak of our Lord. This piece of clothing was probably worn over one shoulder, gathered around the front and back, and tied at the waist. Perhaps she touched just a tassel dangling from its hem. Despite her secretive touch, Jesus chose to bring attention to this very private moment, so He paused and asked a startling question: "Who touched me?" (Luke 8:45, NIV).

No doubt the procession stopped momentarily, and Peter, always willing to give voice to thoughts everyone else was thinking, spoke up and stated the obvious: the crowd was pressing against Jesus from all sides. Jesus calmly replied, "Someone touched me; I know that power has gone out from me" (Luke 8:46, NIV).

At this point in the poignant narrative, three aspects of Christ's decision making in this brief encounter cause anyone who would call himself or herself a servant-leader to ask three questions:

Question one. Am I sensitive to the needs, spoken and unspoken, of those with whom I come in contact, especially those who are different than I am? As busy leaders we are surrounded by people from all dimensions of our ministry and the surrounding community. Because of the danger of falling victim to the tyranny of the urgent, we carefully plan out our day and skillfully manage our time, heeding the advice of seminar instructors: "If you don't manage your time, everyone else will be happy to do that for you." However, have we turned off the receptors through which the Holy Spirit communicates quietly that there are people in our path every day whose names do not appear on our to-do agenda but who are in need of a special touch from the Body of Christ? Have we pulled down the cell tower and stopped receiving calls from those in need in the name of span of control, direct reports, and strategic objectives—three management concepts that administrators are taught about as aids in focusing their efforts and limiting unwanted interruptions and distractions?

Question two. If I identify needs in those around me, do I take the time to care? In this Gospel account Jesus could have simply dispensed His healing power and acknowledged the woman by giving her a glance, a smile, a wink. But He did not—He wanted to cement a relationship with her and to clarify that what had occurred was not the result of a superstitious touch of a tassel but was actually the result of her faith. He wanted this to be her first step in a new experience with the living Lord.

I recall pulling into the school's parking lot one morning just as I did each day, but on this day I didn't turn off the car, because I was enjoying listening to a new Christian artist and wanted to hear the rest of the song. Suddenly my quiet time ended by someone's rapping on my window—and I hadn't even turned off my car! I don't recall whether I greeted the intruder with a smile or not, but it was time to go to work. On the basis of experiences such as this, I want to strongly encourage you to designate times such as during carpool line, bus drop-off, lunchtime, or intervals between classes to simply be available to students, teachers, parents, and community members in general. This visibility and availability strengthen your leadership by communicating your caring and solidify the values you want others to share.

Question three. Most important, am I relying on the power of the Holy Spirit, and thus do I actually have something from the Lord to give to those in need? Most likely everyone reading this chapter who has spent any time at all in ministry knows what it means for us to try to do ministry in our own strength. We often forget Isaiah's instructions: "Those who hope in the Lord will renew their strength. They will soar on wings like eagles; they will run and not grow weary, they will walk and not be faint" (Isaiah 40:31, NIV).

HELMSMAN'S LOG

Popular author and pastor Gene Wilkes has listed seven principles that describe how Jesus led as a servant:
1. Jesus humbled himself and allowed God to exalt him.
2. Jesus followed his Father's will rather than sought a position.
3. Jesus defined greatness as being a servant and being first as becoming a slave.
4. Jesus risked serving others because he trusted that he was God's Son.
5. Jesus left his place at the head table to serve the needs of others.

Helmsman's Log

6. Jesus shared responsibility and authority with those he called to lead.

7. Jesus built a team to carry out a worldwide vision. (1998, 11–12)

After receiving a type of no-confidence vote from a group of deacons at his church, Gene Wilkes spent two weeks in prayer and met with the church leaders again but with a changed heart. A turning point in his ministry occurred as he took a towel and cleaned the shoes of men who had evaluated his ministry as ineffective in their congregation. Wilkes would later reflect on God's blessing his ministry and allowing him to have a successful turnaround: "I learned that the power of leading as a servant comes from God's using a person who humbles himself (on his own or through the actions of others) to God's call on his life and who serves those who were entrusted to him in order to carry out that call. I learned that my greatest test of servant leadership may be to wash the feet of those who have the ability to ask for my resignation. That event has become a watershed in my relationship with God and with Christ's church" (1998, 7). ⚓

THE NEED FOR SERVANT LEADERSHIP TODAY

Do you doubt that you have students in your school who are hurting underneath a cool or expressionless facade? Consider the descriptions of some high-school girls who all played on one team coached by a friend of mine:

+ The first-base player was born to a drug-addicted teen mother and was adopted at an early age. She constantly struggles with her biracial genetic makeup.
+ The second-base player is a country girl with a very hard, distant father. She has anger issues and racial prejudice. Her mother is emotionally and verbally abused also.
+ The third-base player is trying to find a replacement for her father's lack of care and affection. He has bipolar disorder, and he has threatened suicide on several occasions. During the season he disappeared for a week.

- The left fielder's dad and mom divorced when she was only a year old. She can be rebellious and stubborn.
- The center fielder's dad and mom are still together, but her dad had an affair with her mom's best friend a decade ago and produced a child. The dad is a hard drinker, and he uses his moderate wealth to fix problems.
- The right fielder's dad killed himself when she was ten. He shot himself, leaving a note saying the reason was that she didn't love him anymore.
- The catcher is withdrawn and secretive, and she has not opened up to anyone about her dad's accidental overdose of painkillers.
- One of the bench players is worldly and difficult to motivate. Her father is in jail.
- Another bench player's parents are nice, but her dad doesn't think before he speaks to his daughter. He once told her he didn't know why she bothered pitching because she was not good at it. Consequently, she now hates to pitch and refuses to try.
- Still another bench player is a great kid and a hard worker. Her sister died several years ago in a boating accident.

The remaining five players come from homes in which both parents are strong Christians. The coach describes the team chemistry as incredibly positive, and the players support one another in special ways. No doubt he feels a special burden to make each season a special one, a type of oasis, for those players who are dealing with tragedy at home.

Feeling exhausted? Too fatigued to respond to those around you who are hurting, especially members of your own family? Start by reviewing your priorities. Maybe there are too many projects and problems that you feel personally obligated to carry. On the other hand, sometimes leaders accept a lengthy list of responsibilities because they are more comfortable in front of a computer screen than they are with individuals who need a special person to listen to them—a special touch only those leaders can provide.

Are you not really feeling much like a servant? Philippians 2 reminds the followers of Christ about the sacrifice and servant attitude of Christ:

> Make your own attitude that of Christ Jesus, who, existing in the form of God, did not consider equality with God as something to be used for His own

advantage. Instead He emptied Himself by assuming the form of a slave, taking on the likeness of men. And when He had come as a man in His external form, He humbled Himself by becoming obedient to the point of death—even to death on a cross. For this reason God also highly exalted Him and gave Him the name that is above every name, so that at the name of Jesus every knee should bow—of those who are in heaven and on earth and under the earth—and every tongue should confess that Jesus Christ is Lord, to the glory of God the Father. (vv. 5–11, HCSB)

Here we have the well-known kenosis* passage, which explains that Jesus emptied Himself of divine privileges and chose to assume "the form of a slave" (v. 7). The exhortation to "make your own attitude that of Christ Jesus" (v. 5) connects with the imperatives in verses 3 and 4:
+ Do not do anything out of rivalry or conceit.
+ In humility, consider others more important than yourselves.
+ Look out for the interests of others.

Perhaps now is the time to consider setting aside some of the authority and privilege you have been amassing and eagerly look for individuals who need a servant's touch.

---

*The Greek word kenosis is the noun form of kenoo, one of the verbs in Philippians 2:7. According to Young's Analytical Concordance to the Bible, the verb form is "kenoo," which means "to empty" (Young n.d., 809). The New American Standard Bible translates this verb as "emptied" in the phrase "emptied Himself."

Dropping Anchor
Staying Power in the Storm

The greatest survival tactic the leader must employ in the storm

+ The Krakatau eruption, and a helmsman who survived it

+ Sir John Franklin, an explorer who did not adequately prepare

+ Christ, an anchor for administrators

Though most of us will never sail on the Sea of Galilee, we feel as if we have been there because of the compelling stories in the Gospels. This body of water, located 25 to 30 miles from the Mediterranean Sea, is more than 650 feet below the surface of that larger body of water. The rapid descent of cool, dry winds hitting the humid air above the sea is a perfect scenario for strong, violent storms that include fierce winds and waves.

Such was the case on a night after a long day of ministering to citizens of Galilee. As described in Matthew 8:23–27, the storm hit the experienced fishermen quickly, and they were paralyzed by fear as they fought the wind and the waves for control of their sailboat. In the middle of the chaos, Jesus was asleep! It's curious that they chose to awaken the carpenter-turned-teacher. Did they wish Him to be awake before He drowned? His question to them should ring in the ears of every helmsman: "Why are you fearful?" (v. 26, HCSB). The Amplified Bible uses the word *timid*.

Apparently Jesus was challenging them to confront the real problem, which was not the weather but their faith. First, we must have belief, meaning that we believe the right things about God. Second, we must have commitment, the muscle of perseverance that enables belief to shape our lives. Third, we must have trust, which means believing in God even when the physical evidence does not support such an act of the will. If we look at the storms of ministry apart from our faith, we have every reason to fear. But if we look with eyes of faith to the God of our salvation, we can find rest in the midst of the storm. Consider the harrowing events thrust upon the captain of a steamship as he faced certain disaster following one of the most cataclysmic events in the history of the world.

THE KRAKATAU VOLCANO

The natural disaster that occurred in August 1883 may be considered one of the most dramatic displays of nature in the history of our planet, perhaps surpassed only by the Genesis flood. Researchers have estimated that the eruption of Krakatau in the Sunda Strait between Java and Sumatra in Indonesia equaled 13,000 atom bombs exploding simultaneously. People reported hearing the explosion 3,000 miles away in the middle of the Australian Outback to the east and off the coast of Africa to the west. If such an event were to occur in New York City, people in Los Angeles and people in London would hear the sound (Discovery Channel 2006). A decade later in the now-famous painting *The Scream*, Edvard Munch revealed a background of bizarre colors in the sky. Munch was depicting the appearance of the sky in Norway following this catastrophic event (Reuters 2003).

And there was the wave. Entire islands were covered, lighthouses were destroyed, and countless lives were lost, including the lives of people on untold numbers of ships. Experienced mariners and coastal residents may have heard of the ocean's probable reaction to an earthquake or a volcanic eruption, but one helmsman in particular responded with courage and wisdom to the mountain of water that plowed across hundreds of miles of open water, submerging everything in its path. What makes this a riveting narrative for a leadership chapter is the decision making of that helmsman. Captain Lindeman made a strategic decision to leave the apparent security of a harbor and to pilot his ship, the *Loudon*, out to the open sea—where he predicted he would meet the tsunami head-on. He knew that the wave would increase as it moved toward the shore (Discovery Channel 2006).

The bravery and seamanship of Captain Lindeman resulted in the survival of his entire crew and the hundred passengers aboard his ship. Unfortunately, there remain stories of other vessels that experienced the opposite fate. "The wave lifted the steamship *Berouw* up the Koeripan River valley, depositing the ship over a mile inland, thirty feet above sealevel, killing all 28 of its crew members" (Department of Geological Sciences).

So what strategic decisions did Captain Lindeman make in addition to deciding to meet a 100-foot wave head-on? His logbook reveals that first he sent all the passengers and crew to the lowest deck of the ship to help give the vessel the best balance possible. He made this decision in part because the ship would become top-heavy from the rapid buildup of volcanic ash on the ship's upper deck. Second, he ordered the dropping of the ship's anchors to give the large vessel added stability when the bow met the face of the gigantic wave. Third, he ordered the engine room to increase the ship's speed, despite the lowering of the anchors, in order that the ship's momentum might carry the freighter up and over the wave (Discovery Channel 2006). His strategy worked, and this account came from eyewitnesses who survived because of his heroic efforts:

> Suddenly we saw a gigantic wave of prodigious height advancing toward the seashore with considerable speed. Immediately, the crew … managed to set sail in face of the imminent danger; the ship had just enough time to meet with the wave from the front. The ship met the wave head on and the Loudon was lifted up with dizzying rapidity and made a formidable leap.… The ship rode at a high angle over the crest of the wave and down the other side. The wave continued on its journey toward land, and the benumbed crew watched as the sea in a single sweeping motion consumed the town. There, where an instant before had lain the town of Telok Betong, nothing remained but the open sea. (Department of Geological Sciences)

SIR JOHN FRANKLIN

We find a contrast to Captain Lindeman's strategic decision making when we examine Rear Admiral Sir John Franklin's decisions. Sir John Franklin (1786–1847) was a British sea captain and an Arctic explorer whose final expedition disappeared while attempting to navigate and chart the Canadian Arctic's Northwest Passage. The entire crew was lost, and its fate remained a mystery for fourteen years. Even today the answers to many questions remain missing. But some factors in the failure of the dangerous expedition gained clarity from the discoveries of some of Franklin's contemporaries who risked their own lives to try to locate the adventuresome explorer. Three previous expeditions by Franklin, which succeeded in charting much of the Arctic coastline, had earned him much notoriety. As a result of the successful expeditions by Franklin, George IV knighted him. At the urging of several friends, Franklin set off on his final expedition on May 19, 1845. His wife and acquaintances at home in London never heard from him again (Cookman 2000, 1–29). So what possibly caused the demise of the experienced leader? Could the reason have been inadequate preparation for the hardships that lay ahead?

Experienced outdoorsman, researcher, and journalist Scott Cookman reached some conclusions after painstakingly reviewing documents related to the outfitting of the expedition and meticulously comparing the documents' details with the journals of those who uncovered scant evidence while searching for Franklin and his lost expedition: "In the headlong rush to get to sea, decisions that would prove fatal weren't (or couldn't be) properly weighed. Expediency decided things" (2000, 206–8):

- "The decision to fit the ships with bastardized railway engines, not marine locomotives, had grave consequences."
- "Reinforcing the vessels with tons of wood and iron was another fateful decision. There was no time to test the effect the added weight would have on the ships' handling and sailing abilities."
- The production of the canned goods—meats, vegetables, and soups—was "so hurried and rushed that no quality control whatever was practiced." Cookman concludes, "Without doubt, [the canned-goods manufacturer] purposefully delayed delivery of his goods to Franklin's ships until the last possible moment to escape detection."

Oddly, another source lists both the expedition's luxuries that would prove of no use and the tragic, shortsighted decisions not to procure the warmest clothing possible in the eventuality of an overland trek: "Everything possible was done to provide for the health and comfort of the officers and men: heating was supplied by steam-boilers serving a network of pipes; each ship carried huge quantities of the latest patent preserved foods, china, cut glass, and silverware; and large libraries and other educational aids were available. Just the clothing might have seemed inadequate—standard naval cloth supplemented only by underwear and wolf-skin blankets—but then the expedition was not expected to linger in the Arctic" (*Dictionary of Canadian Biography Online* 2000).

Cookman titled his book on this topic *Ice Blink: The Tragic Fate of Sir John Franklin's Lost Polar Expedition*. Realizing his readers' need for an explanation, Cookman defines his esoteric title: *ice blink* is "the name nineteenth-century sailors gave polar mirages, caused by light reflected off the pack ice" (2000, vii). Cookman's thoughts should serve as a sober warning to all of us serving Christ in our calling as educators: Are we depending on anything that is a mirage? Have we placed our confidence in temporal or superficial goals that offer false hope or illusions of success?

CHRIST, THE ANCHOR

Janet Lowrie Nason, an experienced Christian educator and an author, describes the importance of administrators' anchoring themselves in the Lord:

Christian school administrators must be anchored in deep relationship to the immutable God as they face constant change and unexpected problems. They must maintain the imperative relationship with our heavenly Father, who communicates wisdom through His Word. They must balance healthy family relationships and outside activities. The God-given understanding of their position in Christ provides an anchor during the pounding of circumstances, and it enables them to persevere during overwhelming tragedy. A leader with deep spiritual roots may draw on those resources during times of drought and difficulties. Working in Satan's battleground presents a constant challenge. Spiritual warfare that demands spiritual resources becomes a weekly reality. (2002, 11)

HELMSMAN'S LOG

Have you ever put yourself in the place of one of the disciples who accompanied Jesus in the boat the night of the storm? The following is my attempt to see through the eyes of one of the disciples:

Every time He gets in my boat, He teaches me—about His lordship, about fishing and sailing, and about myself. The first time He asked for permission to come aboard it was a beautiful, sunny day, and the lake was completely calm. We had been fishing all day, but with no success. His request made no sense to a tired crew, but we did as He suggested. There was something special about the way He spoke to us. You may have heard what happened next—without explanation our nets were filled to overflowing!

The next time, well, it was a night like we had never seen. The darkness, the wind, the waves frightened us to the point of panic and then despair. And Jesus was asleep! I'm not sure why we woke Him up—what was a carpenter going to contribute? Perhaps we thought He just might have an answer.

Helmsman's Log

This last time surpassed the previous experiences and left me believing that there isn't anything He can't do—Himself or with me! This time He put me in the most difficult, challenging situation yet, but He was right there with me, and He demonstrated His control of this and any situation when He spoke. ⚓

Administrator, recall the most recent storm in your ministry. Did the storm toss you around with the deck furniture, and did you simply hang on for dear life? Did the crisis shake you to your core and make you question your own leadership or even the direction of your ministry? Like the explorer Sir John Franklin, have you failed to bring along those things that are essential for your survival and success? The author of Hebrews makes use of the metaphor of an anchor when he describes the confidence we have in Christ: "We have this hope as an anchor for the soul, firm and secure" (6:19, NIV).

New Testament scholar Donald Guthrie describes this brief but powerful verse and explains the depth of insight the author of Hebrews provides for his readers:

Meditating on the theme of hope leads him to comment on certain striking characteristics of hope. The first is its immovability which is vividly illustrated by the figure of an *anchor*. Nowhere else in the New Testament is this used in a metaphorical way. It is a rich image. The job of the anchor is to remain fixed in the sea-bed whatever the conditions at sea. Indeed the rougher the weather the more important is the anchor for the stability and safety of the boat. It is an apt symbol of Christian hope. It was, in fact, used graphically as a symbol among early Christians, and was frequently linked with the fish symbol. It is surprising that no other New Testament writer makes use of it. Perhaps it is too fanciful to suggest that the writer had had experience at sea and had personally learned to value the anchor in times of danger. According to the RSV it is the anchor which is described as *sure and steadfast*, but the adjectives could refer to the hope. It makes little difference to the meaning. The first adjective means "safe" (*asphalē*), incapable of being moved. The second (*bebaian*), secure in itself, is practically a synonym of the other. It is translated in 3:6 and 3:14 as "confidence." In New Testament thought generally, as here, confidence and hope are closely tied. (1983, 153; italics in original)

There's a pedestrian bridge that crosses the mighty Niagara River at a point where many locals use the river for recreation. But all do so with the understanding that the water can carry unsuspecting boaters downstream to Horseshoe Falls, the destination of many sightseers and the place where millions of gallons of water a minute go hurtling over that part of Niagara Falls. Legend has it that attached to the footbridge is a sign visible only to boaters that says, "Do you have an anchor?" Farther on, there's supposedly a second sign; it asks, "Do you know how to use it?" The spiritual application is obvious—is your ministry anchored on the Rock and on Him alone? Confidence and hope in the Lord Jesus will give you staying power in the storms of leadership.

Designing with Integrity
Making Sure of the Essentials

6

The dimension of leadership that defines the leader

+ The *Vasa* tragedy
+ The apostle Paul and others on integrity
+ Old Testament people who failed the test of integrity
+ Lessons from King David on integrity
+ Hardship and integrity
+ Finances and integrity
+ Trust and integrity
+ Survival or collapse in the perfect storm
+ The *Titanic's* lack of integrity

S oundness. *Completeness.* *Wholeness.* In design. In planning. In execution. No one knew that a ship named the *Vasa* possessed none of these qualities, but people soon found out....

THE TRAGEDY OF THE VASA

In the early seventeenth century, young King Gustavus II Adolphus of Sweden needed to build a navy to complete his military triumphs. Poland and Sweden were at war, and Sweden had lost twelve ships in quick succession. King Gustavus Adolphus ordered new warships, among them the *Vasa*—replete with a total of 700 sculptures and ornaments designed to degrade Sweden's enemies and impress the world (Vasa Museum n.d.a, n.d.b).

But the *Vasa*, intended to be the world's mightiest warship, would not impress anyone because its construction lacked soundness and integrity. The skilled shipbuilder Henrik Hybertsson oversaw the construction of the *Vasa*, but he became too ill to oversee the work directly, and then he died a year before the work was complete. His successor had no written record of the construction, and the king was pushing him to finish the job in half the normal time. "Although seventeenth century sailing ships demanded complex construction, building practices look primitive by today's standards. The master shipwright held the plans for a ship in his head. No scientifically determined measurements guided construction" (Badertscher 2000–2001).

The *Vasa* also lacked soundness because the king demanded more guns than the original plan called for, and thus the *Vasa* included an unprecedented second gun deck. "Forty-eight 24 pound cannons, each weighing one and a half tons, plus 24 smaller guns, strained the balance of the ship" (Badertscher 2000–2001). Having 64 guns in total and a hull that was too narrow, the *Vasa*'s rushed construction spelled danger (Vasa Museum n.d.a, n.d.c).

Inquiries later revealed that a test of the ship's stability took place before its maiden voyage. Thirty men ran back and forth across the ship's deck when she was moored at the quay. They had to stop after three runs, however, because the ship almost capsized. The test was not nearly complete. Admiral Klas Fleming was present, but he did not stop the ship from sailing. The king was in Polish

Prussia waiting impatiently, and he had approved the ship's dimensions (Vasa Museum n.d.c). The ship was destined for a watery grave, but no one would have guessed the timing and the setting of this tragedy.

Vera Marie Badertscher pictures the events unfolding:

On a glorious summer day, small boats towed the great ship from her mooring near the castle. With gold ornaments flashing sunlight, she fired a farewell salute and hundreds of people on the banks watched as she set sail.

Within a few minutes after sails were hoisted, a gust of wind tilted the ship, but it righted itself. Along the embankments, the people gasped. Then they covered their faces as a second gust of wind dropped over the inland hills. The ship listed again. The gun ports, still open from the farewell salute, filled with water and the Vasa slowly disappeared beneath 110 feet of water, flags and sails still flying. She had traveled only 1400 yards. (2000–2001)

Every leader's blood should run cold from reading that account of the sudden and deadly collapse of an elegant and powerful sailing ship. Could that happen to your school? Could that happen in your personal life?

INSIGHTS ON INTEGRITY

Paul knew that his fellow soldier in spiritual warfare would be attacked and tempted throughout the battle and that integrity and stability were essential if Timothy was going to survive and succeed. We must pay heed to Paul's exhortation to Timothy: "This command I entrust to you, Timothy, my son, in accordance with the prophecies previously made concerning you, that by them you fight the good fight, keeping faith and a good conscience, which some have rejected and suffered shipwreck in regard to their faith" (1 Timothy 1:18–19).

Paul's inspired wording here is especially instructive considering the preceding nautical story. Getting rid of our faith or our good conscience even for a few moments will threaten to shipwreck us, just as the instability of the *Vasa* led to its doom. We have witnessed it all too often:

+ A pastor commingles church and school funds, and money disappears.
+ An administrator fails to deal decisively with a sexual scandal among his staff.
+ A headmaster intimidates his staff when his actions are questioned and camouflages his misdeeds from his board.

+ Board members face pressure to make a hurried decision absent all the important details and sufficient time for prayer.
+ A coach uses ineligible players in a championship game.

Paul warned his co-laborer Titus about the pressures of participating in ministry when he wrote, "Likewise urge the young men to be sensible; in all things show yourself to be an example of good deeds, with purity in doctrine, dignified, sound in speech which is beyond reproach, so that the opponent will be put to shame, having nothing bad to say about us" (Titus 2:6–8). In verse 7 the word *purity* can mean "integrity," "soundness," or "incorruption." Paul reminds us about what we have no doubt seen in our lives: when we are sensible, we do not provide our critics with more ammunition to lob at us—they will have nothing to talk about and will be put to shame.

Helmsman's Log

Following a much-needed expansion of the school's facilities and playing fields, a school leader was blindsided by false accusations and gossip about excessive noise, unreasonable traffic problems, and lights from stadium use in the evenings. He methodically researched each accusation and reviewed the neighbors' complaints, the school's policies and practices, and any relevant local laws. This gracious and methodical approach produced some new traffic patterns on the part of students, parents, and vendors. He reminded the school's critics that the buffer the school had created by using plants and trees in its landscaping of the new areas exceeded all public policies by 200 percent. And ironically he could report that the nighttime lighting tests revealed that the streetlight in front of the main accuser's house produced significantly more ambient light than did the stadium lights, whose ambient light was well below the local codes. ⚓

Nationally known Christian educator Kenn Gangel provides today's administrators and leaders with these biblical insights:

> The book of Proverbs alone among all the books of the Bible uses the word *integrity* (as translated in the NIV) five times. Proverbs 13:6 tells us that "righteousness guards the man of integrity, but wickedness overthrows the sinner." We find similar words in Proverbs 11:3: "The integrity of the upright guides them, but the unfaithful are destroyed by their duplicity." Now here we have a word we can get our hands on. *Duplicity* clearly means deliberately saying one thing to one person and something quite different to another. It is deceptiveness, or double dealing, and it literally comes from the old Latin word *duplex*, which we still commonly use today. A two-faced person, whose heart is not rooted in righteousness, will eventually show his true persona by demonstrating a self in whom two separate houses have been built. (2005–2006, 6)

And from the New Testament Gangel provides these insights: "The appearance of the word *adialeiptos* in Titus 2 is very much contextually interpreted. This is a teaching chapter, and verses seven and eight could not be clearer: 'In everything set them an example by doing what is good. In your teaching show integrity, seriousness and soundness of speech that cannot be condemned, so that those who oppose you may be ashamed because they have nothing bad to say about us.' These imperatives are a direct challenge to Titus himself, and they have to do with the way he demonstrated leadership with integrity through teaching" (2005–2006, 6).

In the book *Trust: The One Thing That Makes or Breaks a Leader*, Les Csorba, former special assistant for presidential personnel in the G. H. W. Bush administration, argues that all leadership depends on trust: "*The real leader inspires trust and action among followers. His leadership is character in motion with trust as its fuel*" (2004, xv; italics in original). He continues, "Leadership is built on many characteristics such as humility, service, vision, courage, and so on, but, fundamentally, leadership is built on trust. You cannot sit on a broken chair. Neither can a leader lead without sitting on a seat of trust. The trust that is so slow to form in leadership can come apart so very quickly" (xxiv).

Pursuing Csorba's concept, leaders of Christian schools must ask themselves, "When my leadership depends on people's trust in me—when I have to make a very difficult personnel decision and cannot make the reasons known, when it is time for change and some faithful teachers just don't see it—on what basis can I ask these members of my learning community to trust me?" I deeply believe that the only basis for legitimate trust, as opposed to blind trust or reckless followership, is integrity. I believe that *trust* is a word used to characterize something that exists in a relationship between two or more people. The genesis of this trust is integrity within leaders, and their character generates this integrity. A diagram of this truth may be as follows:

Character ⇒ Integrity ⇒ Trust ⇒ Effective Leadership

Integrity of practice is the linchpin that connects the character of people to their effectiveness as leaders.

J. Robert "Bobby" Clinton, author of *The Making of a Leader: Recognizing the Lessons and Stages of Leadership Development*, agrees with this relationship between character and integrity in his discussion of what he has called "the integrity check":

> At the heart of any assessment of biblical qualifications for leadership lies the concept of integrity—that uncompromising adherence to a code of moral, artistic, or other values that reveals itself in sincerity, honesty, and candor and avoids deception or artificiality.... The God-given capacity to lead has two parts: giftedness and character. Integrity is the heart of character.
>
> An emerging leader becomes aware of the importance of integrity through integrity checks. An integrity check is a test that God uses to evaluate intentions in order to shape character. This check is a springboard to an expanded sphere of influence. There are three parts to an integrity check: the challenge to consistency with inner convictions, the response to the challenge, and the resulting expansion of ministry. (1988, 30–31)

OLD TESTAMENT CHARACTERS LACKING INTEGRITY

Men who lacked integrity in their decision making and behavior abound in the Old Testament. Father Abraham, "the friend of God" (James 2:23), chose to lie when the possibility of dying at the hands of the Egyptians confronted him because of his wife's beauty. (Some early commentators speculated that Abraham's father had two wives and that Sarah was born to the second wife, a situation that would have made her Abraham's half sister; but even if that had been the case, Abraham was still being deceptive by giving the impression that she was his full sister.) Though both he and Sarah were spared, serious consequences resulted from his lack of honesty. It is important to note that

Abraham was living in the will of God but that his faith and character faced testing when there came a famine in the land (Genesis 12:10–20). How many administrators risk the integrity of their ministry when there comes a "famine" in their cash flow? We all know the temptation to misrepresent the realities of the budget in order to pressure the board to approve a new expenditure.

Another more tragic example is found in the life of King Saul. Following his victory over the Amalekites, Saul disobeyed the Lord's command regarding Amalek: "Utterly destroy all that he has, and do not spare him; but put to death both man and woman, child and infant, ox and sheep, camel and donkey" (1 Samuel 15:3). Then the king added dishonesty and deception to the list of failures in the subsequent confrontation with Samuel. Not just once or twice, but three times! And when Saul decided to come clean, his excuse was that he had "feared the people and listened to their voice" (1 Samuel 15:24). Then he heard these chilling words from Samuel: "I will not return with you; for you have rejected the word of the Lord, and the Lord has rejected you from being king over Israel" (1 Samuel 15:26). When we are caught in a storm of opinion and conflicting advice, to whose voice will we listen?

HELMSMAN'S LOG

Do you ever find yourself saying, "Here's my decision, but don't tell anyone." I made it an important matter of practice, with some scar tissue to show for it, never to utter those words. When confronted with the daily nuances of policy interpretation, I always tried to say, "Here's my decision, and when someone asks, here are the reasons that I am choosing to make an exception to the policy." Please note that I said *when* and not *if*. It was not that everything I decided was of importance; it was that I never naively thought I was making decisions in a vacuum. When a longtime staff member asked to be excused for two weeks to serve as a chaperone and accompany a school family on a luxury cruise, I decided that it was warranted because of his seniority and modest living style, as well as the overall dependability of the students in

HELMSMAN'S LOG

his classes that would need to have a long-term substitute. After working out the arrangements with the board for him to take leave without pay, I explained my reasoning completely to the rest of the faculty. Would all principals make the same decision? Probably not, but at least my faculty could depend on me to be completely transparent with them. ⚓

I believe that one of the key factors in the shipwrecks that occur in ministry is the tolerance of small fissures that arise in our character—a tolerance that then leads to failure of integrity in our decision making and failure in communication with others in our learning community. The major place this occurs is between the head of school and the board. Like the weaknesses in the design of the *Vasa*, these seemingly harmless flaws in our relationships with the people we report to will ultimately lead to the certain weakening or even destruction of our ministries.

THE INTEGRITY OF KING DAVID

King David, though a man who certainly made some horrendous decisions, shows today's leaders some qualities of integrity:

Respect for authority. Even secretly cutting Saul's robe bothered David's conscience; an alternate translation is, "David's heart struck him" (1 Samuel 24:5, ESV). So David vowed not to touch the man who tried so desperately to kill him, and David persuaded all his men to follow his example and not to raise a hand against Saul (1 Samuel 24:5–15). I passionately believe that much of the friction that occurs in the relationships between the leaders of Christian schools would cease if all those in authority would be "heart struck" when they attack or quarrel with those the Lord has put into place.

Recognition of God's control. On another night David was once again in a position to kill his adversary, and he convinced his commandos to spare Saul's life. The reason for David's decision making and actions was clear: David believed that the Lord was in control. "As the Lord lives, surely the Lord will strike him, or his day will come that he dies, or he will go down into battle and perish" (1 Samuel 26:10). Please don't misunderstand: I am not suggesting that we pray for the demise of those who thwart our ideas and plans, but we must joyfully accept that the Lord placed them in their positions and that He is not taken by surprise when there are disagreements and delays. Can we not say that some Christian leaders conduct themselves as practical atheists—giving no evidence that they believe the Lord is sovereign?

Responsibility for sin and repentance. Fissures occur in the strongest rock formations. Sin occurs in the lives of the greatest leaders. How do men and women of integrity react when their character has failed? David demonstrated that to us after an incredible collapse that included seduction, adultery, lying, and murder. When his friend Nathan confronted him, David responded, "I have sinned against the Lord" (2 Samuel 12:13). Immediately Nathan responded, "The Lord also has taken away your sin; you shall not die. However, because by this deed you have given occasion to the enemies of the Lord to blaspheme, the child also that is born to you shall surely die" (vv. 13–14). The fissures closed. God's grace prevailed, but once again the Lord's enemies had something about which to gossip and blaspheme. How many opportunities for students to receive Christ do leaders forfeit as a result of sinful struggles at the highest levels of our schools?

Request for wholeness. In Psalm 51 King David penned a contrite sinner's prayer of pardon. Leaders of integrity will recognize that they must paradoxically be completely broken before the Lord for wholeness to be restored. "The sacrifices of God are a broken spirit; a broken and a contrite heart, O God, You will not despise" (v. 17). David also recognized that God's power could make him whole again: "Create in me a clean heart, O God, and renew a steadfast spirit within me. Do not cast me away from Your presence and do not take Your Holy Spirit from me. Restore to me the joy of Your salvation and sustain me with a willing spirit. Then I will teach transgressors Your ways, and sinners will be converted to You" (vv. 10–13).

Remembering promises. David demonstrated a fifth quality of integrity when he remembered the commitment he made to Jonathan before ascending to the throne of Jonathan's father, Saul. Years earlier during the time that King Saul pursued David and sought to kill him, a deep friendship developed between Jonathan and David. As Jonathan risked his own life for his friend, David made a covenant to remember his friend's entire family by protecting them and providing for them. Once David's leadership and administration were firmly established, he remembered this covenant and asked, "Is there yet anyone left of the house of Saul, that I may show him kindness for Jonathan's sake?" (2 Samuel 9:1). A servant introduced David to Jonathan's son, Mephibosheth, a young man who was "crippled in both feet" (v. 3). David made good on his promise by restoring to Mephibosheth all the land of Mephibosheth's grandfather and by inviting Mephibosheth to be a regular guest at his table; this member of the house of Saul was treated "as one of the king's sons" (v. 11).

HELMSMAN'S LOG

How do young leaders become people of integrity who are prepared to weather the storms of leadership? Recall the model that described the relationship between character and trust, with integrity as the linchpin (see page 78). Leadership begins with character development. Scripture has much to say about this development, and James 1:2–4 clearly expresses the process of forging character: "Consider it all joy, my brethren, when you encounter various trials, knowing that the testing of your faith produces endurance. And let endurance have its perfect result, so that you may be perfect and complete, lacking in nothing."

Here the author references the familiar process of heating precious metal to remove the impurities. This testing yields endurance, and the result of endurance is a character that is mature and complete. Later in that chapter James returns to this concept when he writes, "Blessed is a man who perseveres under trial" (v. 12). ⚓

INTEGRITY FORGED THROUGH HARDSHIP

Don't run from a storm or hide below deck—face it, and God will use it to do a great work in you. Remember these words of Job: "But He knows the way I take; when He has tried me, I shall come forth as gold" (Job 23:10).

Les Csorba writes, "*Moral character is forged in the testing of integrity and fire of our sufferings*" (2004, 223; italics in original). He goes on to explain that trusted leaders are cast from the crucible of their experiences. To illustrate, Csorba describes President Lincoln and the incredible hardships he faced before becoming one of the greatest leaders our nation has ever known:

> President Lincoln was perhaps more refined by the unrelenting flame of suffering than any other American president. He was driven out of his early family home at age seven, forced to work to support his family, lost his mother at age nine, lost his job as a store clerk at age twenty-two, went into debt at age twenty-three, and was turned down for marriage by his long-time girlfriend.
>
> He was defeated time and time again for election to the Congress; at forty-one, he lost his four-year-old son; at forty-five, he ran for the Senate, but lost; at forty-seven, he was defeated for the vice-presidential nomination, and at forty-nine, he ran for the Senate again and lost. At fifty-one, he became the president of the United States. It was one of Lincoln's former critics, Edwin Stanton, who said of Lincoln at the time of his death, "There lies the most perfect ruler of men the world has ever seen … [and] now he belongs to the ages." (224)

FINANCIAL INTEGRITY

Loss of trust due to lack of integrity in financial dealings can quickly cripple or completely disable a ministry. This book is not the place for listing and discussing financial procedures known as GAAP (generally accepted accounting procedures), but a strong exhortation for the highest level of integrity in our financial dealings is in order here. One of the best concepts to ensure this integrity is a simple commitment to accountability. Paul established this means to integrity in his correspondence with the Corinthians as he discussed with them their participation in a strategic fund collection for the impoverished saints in Jerusalem. In 2 Corinthians 8 Paul described Titus and two other brothers he was sending to receive the Corinthians' donation. While we have a multitude of ways today to verify the credibility of individuals and track the depositing of money, Paul needed to depend on what we call "the rule of two," the establishment of accountability based on the constant presence of two or more individuals who can verify the amount and transactions of a ministry's financial dealings. Today we can institute such practices as setting up purchase-order procedures, undergoing internal and external audits, and having two check signers. In the first century, Paul took great pains to describe the dependability of these three saints who would be handling the money bags. He summarized his commitment in verse 21: "For we are taking pains to do what is right, not only in the eyes of the Lord but also in the eyes of men" (NIV).

We do not have to look far for examples of poor money-handling procedures as well as of outright thievery:

+ A pastor leads the school board to combine its budget with the church's funds, a practice called commingling of funds. Just a few years later $300,000 is missing, along with the pastor.
+ A pastor insists that he sign every check and oversee finances of both the church and the school. Federal withholding for school employees is overlooked, and the local newspaper reveals that the ministry owes the IRS more than $150,000 in back payroll taxes.
+ A school raises money for one purpose, but because of a budget shortfall, the school spends those designated funds in the general operating budget— unethical at best and usually illegal. Such activity can severely threaten a school's tax-exempt status.
+ A school commits another frequent error—allowing parents to work off tuition fees by performing duties around the campus in exchange for reduced tuition. The IRS deems this practice bartering—illegal bartering.
+ Against policy and without the board's knowledge, a head of school approves expenditures not previously discussed or included in the budget, because he believes the money will be well spent or justifiable.

As a young administrator I requested the use of a school credit card, a practice taken for granted today. Every month when the receipts and statement arrived in the mail, before the practice of online posting became popular, I sat down with a board member who was a retired businessman, and we reviewed every purchase. Because I knew that the day of accountability was coming each month, I never gave in to the temptation to treat myself to lunch or purchase a tank of gas for my personal use. I committed myself "to do what [was] right, not only in the eyes of the Lord but also in the eyes of men."

INSPIRING OTHERS TO TRUST

One of the most frequently cited books in current management literature is Patrick Lencioni's *Five Dysfunctions of a Team: A Leadership Fable* (2002), a book about the spiraling destruction that occurs in group dynamics when there is a lack of trust. One review of this influential book summarizes the author's thesis in this way: "In short, Lencioni posits that most teams are dysfunctional because of an absence of trust, which leads to a fear of conflict, which then leads to a lack of commitment. The logical result is avoidance of accountability and, ultimately, inattention to results" (Johnson and Edgren 2006–2007, 14). Janeal Goering, assistant director of the ACSI South-Central Region, comments regarding a related book by Lencioni, "In the opening pages, he clearly identifies the need for teamwork and explains the benefits of an effective, cohesive team. The effectiveness of a team is defined as accomplishing the results that it set out to achieve. There are two key questions that must be asked of any team at the outset: 'Are we really a team?' and 'Are we ready for heavy lifting?' The answers to these two questions invigorate the team to achieve the very best. Lencioni is quick to point out that although achieving teamwork is difficult, it is not complicated" (2006–2007, 15).

Even though the writers of these two reviews describe biblical intersections and express agreements with Lencioni's concepts, they do not question from where this trust comes. In Lencioni's fictional narrative, the new executive challenges his team to be vulnerable and transparent with their teammates. Goering asserts, "Since trust is the foundation of teamwork, it is an essential element for an effective team. Building trust and then maintaining it require both vulnerability and time. Once trust has been gained, it becomes the foundation for mastering conflict" (2006–2007, 15). While it may be too nuanced to argue that trust cannot be the foundation without integrity of leadership, I believe strongly that integrity in the leadership relationship is essential for followers to show vulnerability.

FACING THE PERFECT STORM

In recent years, one of the most famous events concerning a ship in crisis occurred during October 1991 off the Newfoundland coast in an area of the Atlantic known as the Grand Banks. The 72-foot fishing vessel the *Andrea Gail* left Gloucester, Massachusetts, hoping for one last large payday as the season for swordfish came

Helmsman's Log

Let's consider a ship's design for integrity and stability:

The ability of a boat to clear her decks is one of the most crucial aspects of her design. A boarding sea is like putting a swimming pool on the deck; the boat wallows, loses her steerage, and for a few moments is in extreme danger....

If you look out the porthole and see whitewater, you're still near the surface and relatively safe. If you see greenwater, at least you're in the body of the wave. If you see blackwater, you're a submarine....

... Two forces are locked in combat for a ship ...: the downward push of gravity and the upward lift of buoyancy. Gravity is the combined weight of the vessel and everything on it ... seeking the center of the earth. Buoyancy is the force of all the enclosed air in the hull trying to rise above water level.

On a trim and stable ship, these two forces are equal and cancel each other out along the centerline; but all this changes when a boat gets shoved over onto her side. Instead of being lined up, the two forces are now laterally offset. The center of gravity stays where it is, but the center of buoyancy migrates to the submerged side, where proportionally more air has been forced below the waterline. With gravity pushing down at the center and

to a close. The weather at that time of year was always uncertain, but no one could have predicted what was coming: the perfect storm, a convergence of tropical air from the remnants of Hurricane Grace coming from the south, a winter storm off the coast of Sable Island, and high barometric pressure from Canada. The result was a deadly storm that produced waves 100 feet high and claimed many lives, including those of the *Andrea Gail's* crew (Junger 1997).

Helmsman's Log

buoyancy pushing up from the submerged side, the ship pivots on her center and returns to an even keel.... The lateral distance between [the force of gravity and the force of buoyancy] is called the *righting arm*, and the torque they generate is called the *righting moment*. Boats want a big righting moment. They want something that will right them from extreme angles of heel.

The righting moment has three main implications. First of all, the wider the ship, the more stable she is.... The opposite is also true: The taller the ship, the more likely she is to capsize.... Finally, there always comes a point where the boat can no longer right herself. Logically, this would happen when her decks have gone past vertical and the center of gravity falls *outside* the center of buoyancy—the "zero-moment" point. (Junger 1997, 77–79; italics in original)

We can suggest many analogies here, but mainly the question at hand for educators and administrators is whether or not their schools have the integrity of design and stability to withstand the storms that will certainly come. Will your school have the righting moment it needs when crisis hits? When a zero-moment point occurs, will the school's stability be restored, or will the school go under? ⚓

We will probably never know for certain about the final moments of their lives and the details that led to the destruction of the ship, but a great deal of research by journalist Sebastian Junger has revealed some frightening realities about the condition of the ship. Consider the following description of the ship's repair in 1986: "When the *Andrea Gail* was overhauled in 1986, Bob Brown [the ship's owner] simply pulled her out of the water and started welding; no stability tests were performed, no marine architect was consulted. In the trade this is known as 'eyeball engineering,' and it includes the *Andrea Gail* in an overwhelming majority of the commercial fleet that has been altered without plans. The work was done at St. Augustine Trawlers in St. Augustine, Florida; in all, eight tons of machinery and structural changes were added to the boat, including the fuel and water drums on her whaleback deck" (1997, 81).

In a storm that no one could have predicted, the ship's stability and design were not reliable; the ship lacked integrity when it needed to be at its best. How about your personal integrity and the integrity of your school? Are there hidden design flaws? The research of Junger (1997) and his interviews of experienced helmsmen and crews reveal repeated references to rogue waves—walls of water that can appear out of nowhere and inflict massive destruction before the crew members even know what hit them. In addition to possessing needed training, experience, and vigilance, are your leadership and ministry prepared at their foundations to face a hit by an unexpected accusation or scandal? Consider the following examples of changes in a school's design or personnel that could have a weakening influence on the ministry's integrity:

+ A school hires a staff member who offers exceptional giftedness in an area of need but who doesn't support the school's statement of faith.
+ A school incorporates curriculum changes that appear academically attractive but do not fit the school's educational philosophy or its goal of biblical integration.
+ A head of school excuses immoral behavior by a staff member because of lack of courage or fear of reprisals.
+ An administrator secretly spends money or allocates funds not included in the budget without the board's knowledge.
+ A school leader ignores policy procedures that are difficult or unpopular.

Is there a conflict in your mind regarding complete transparency and aboveboard decision making? Perhaps the warring parties are authority versus submission. Yes, you have a broad-based authority to make day-to-day decisions, but the struggles come because you have not clearly articulated to the board what the school's best practices are and have not sought the board's support in codifying those practices as a part of the school's policies and procedures.

Some will read these warnings and imagine that their vessel is superior in size and seaworthiness and that they need not be concerned. The following is a part of the report by a Canadian observer placed on board a Japanese fishing vessel, the *Eishin Maru*, which experienced the perfect storm some 200 miles from the *Andrea Gail*. Judith Reeves was there to make sure that the Japanese crew followed Canadian fishing regulations, and she described the damage done to the long-liner that measured 150 feet, twice the size of the swordfish vessel. Waves were burying the deck. The storm hit the vessel midday on October 29, and by midnight the sustained wind speeds were fifty knots, gusts were hitting sixty, and peak wave heights were over 100 feet (Junger 1997). Reeves then realized the ship was going down:

> We had no steerage and we were right in the eye of the storm....It was a confused sea, all the waves were coming from different directions. The wind was picking up the tops of the waves and slinging them so far that when the search-and-rescue plane arrived, we couldn't even see it. The whole vessel would get shoved over on its side, so that we were completely upside-down. If you get hit by one wave and then hit by another, you can drive the vessel completely down into the water. And so that second before the vessel starts to come up you're just holding your breath, waiting. (130)

I know the experience of fighting off panic in difficult seas. As I drove to the location of the bus accident that morning during my principalship in Maryland, I was most certainly holding my breath. Instead of seeing the usual waves of cars in the oncoming lanes, I was stunned to see not one approaching automobile. As my car drove unimpeded on a major artery that was always flooded with traffic, I imagined how bad the accident must have been to cause such an interruption. Like short electrical bursts of information crossing my mind's eye, I reviewed all the procedures and legalities involved with that situation: the commercial driver's license and background search of the driver, regular bus inspections and scheduled maintenance, insurance for all persons and property involved, regular safety reviews with the passengers including emergency evacuation procedures. Had we taken any shortcuts? Did any of our procedures lack integrity? This was our rogue wave, and I must admit that the blood had completely drained from my face by the time I arrived. What I saw, my eyes could not comprehend: our 45-passenger school bus had clipped and broken a utility pole, and a passenger car's top was totally crushed. My knees buckled, and I had trouble standing. Fortunately for me at that moment the media that had started to gather did not identify me as the leader of the school to which the bus belonged. By God's grace I was able to right myself and quietly care for the driver and our students. Public buses took all our students to local hospitals for observation and for any necessary treatment.

Have this chapter's Scriptures, literature, and nautical stories caught your attention? The Canadian observer along with the Japanese fishermen aboard the *Eishin Maru* survived the perfect storm, but all were lost on the *Andrea Gail*. In the case of the bus collision, thanks to the driver's training that our teacher had received, he kept control of the bus after it had been struck on its side by a sedan driven by an elderly person who was miraculously protected and who fully recovered. The older students remembered our evacuation procedures we had rehearsed just two weeks before and assisted all the younger students in deboarding the bus. And all our documentation was in place. My breathing returned to normal after two days.

Many of the soldiers and sailors on the *Vasa* were not so fortunate. Of the 150 people on board for its inaugural voyage, between 30 and 50 of them died in the disaster. In 1961 when the ship was salvaged, archaeologists found what remained of 25 skeletons (Vasa Museum n.d.a).

THE WEAKNESS OF THE *TITANIC*

William J. Broad's article "In Weak Rivets, a Possible Key to *Titanic*'s Doom" (*New York Times*, April 15, 2008) describes the doom of another ship whose construction lacked soundness and integrity. In the early 1900s, Harland and Wolff, a major shipbuilder in Northern Ireland, acted on its lofty ambitions to construct the three biggest ships in the world—all at the same time. Each ship would require three million rivets, which would act like glue to hold each ship together. But this demand severely strained two resources: material for the rivets and the riveters who welded it.

Research has revealed that members of the company's board expressed great concern in meeting after meeting over a variety of problems related to rivets. During these meetings the board made four critical decisions. First, because of the shortage, they chose to include smaller forges in addition to their usual suppliers. This inclusion often meant less skill and experience. Second, they chose to purchase iron rated number 3 bar, or "best," instead of the highest-quality iron—number 4 bar, known as "best-best." Third, they hired less-experienced riveters to keep pace with the work schedule. What is not widely known is that the responsibility of a riveter required great skill—the riveter had to heat the iron to a precise red cherry color and beat the iron with the right combination of hammer blows.

The board's fourth crucial decision involved the potential to change to steel rivets, which were stronger and able to be installed by machines that improved workmanship. Harland and Wolff chose steel rivets, but only for the ship's central hull, where the stresses were expected to be the most serious. They chose iron rivets, made from inferior material and installed by means of questionable workmanship, for the stern and the bow of the *Titanic*. The bow struck an iceberg at 11:40 PM on April 14, 1912, and the ship sank in just over two and a half hours. Most researchers agree that the gashes in the ship were relatively small but that the pressure of water forced the rivets to give way. And once the rivets gave way, the ship sank much faster. The result is history—1,500 passengers lost their lives.

The *Titanic* was packed with luxury: cafés, squash courts, a swimming pool, Turkish baths, a barbershop, and three libraries. A brochure boasted that the luxury liner was "designed to be unsinkable." This may have been true except for the glue: the rivets—they lacked integrity.

How many families in your school and the wider community are depending on the integrity of your ministry? Are you willing to risk the education, the spiritual development, or even the eternal salvation of even one of these families because of a lack of integrity on your part?

Soundness. Completeness. Wholeness. Are you prepared for the storms?

The Skills of the Helmsman
Techniques Needed to Train a Crew and Prepare for Battle

Training the Crew
Mentoring in the Maelstrom

The most important duty the leader must perform for his or her crew

♦ Moses' model of mentoring: The training of Joshua

♦ A model of leadership development: Personalized leadership

♦ The development of England's greatest naval hero: Admiral Lord Nelson

♦ Two-to-three-minute walk-through observations

♦ Fifteen-minute informal observations

The hit movie *Master and Commander*, featuring the fearless leadership of nineteenth-century naval officer Jack Aubrey, is based on the first book in Patrick O'Brian's best-selling Aubrey/Maturin series. Leading up to the dramatic climax of the story in which Lucky Jack's ship defeats a superior French frigate, the movie includes several poignant scenes in which Captain Aubrey moves through the crew, assigning significant tasks to officers and midshipmen. When a young trainer learns he will not be a member of the boarding party—crew members on the British ship who will be jumping onto the French ship to subdue her crew by hand-to-hand combat—he asks the captain if he can speak with the captain about the assignment. Despite the urgency to continue preparation, the captain pauses to listen to the midshipman's request, and then Jack Aubrey responds, "I know what you want to say. My answer is no. You'll lead your gun crew, and then when we board, you'll take command of the ship from here on the quarterdeck. Do I make myself clear?" The young sailor's face lights up, and he responds, "Take command of the ship! Thank you, sir!" (Weir and Collee 2003).

Though Patrick O'Brian's writing is considered historical fiction, this scene impressed upon me the significant opportunities we have to train and empower staff members, even in the heat of battle!

A Model for Mentoring

One of the most significant transfers of power in the history of humankind would take place in the coming years. The Lord had raised up Moses and equipped him in both ordinary and extraordinary ways. But his days of leadership would one day come to an end.

The Lord had special plans for Joshua, the man He had chosen, and He gave specific instructions for Moses to mentor his replacement. One especially interesting moment occurred after Moses sent Joshua into battle against a mighty foe that was attacking Israel. Following the Israelite victory, the Lord gave very precise instructions to the aging leader. "The Lord said to Moses, 'Write this in a book as a memorial and recite it to Joshua, that I will utterly blot out the memory of Amalek from under heaven'" (Exodus 17:14). The verb *recite* here can be translated "place in the ears of," and it helps paint a vivid picture of the mentoring relationship between Moses and Joshua. It also indicates the importance the Lord placed on the message. The significance of this message may be lost on a modern reader, but it certainly would not have been on Joshua. Deuteronomy 25:18 explains to the Israelites what Amalek had done: "He met you along the way and attacked among you all the stragglers at your rear when you were faint and weary; and he did not fear God." No doubt the Lord's solemn promise would encourage the heart of the young commander in the future when he would face the enemy again.

How about in your administration? Has the Lord led you to prepare a younger educator for future challenges? I believe a part of the stewardship of every leader is that he or she must constantly look for opportunities to recite in the presence of others—to download to their mental iPods—what the Lord has been doing in the ministry and to share with them the vision for the future.

Here are some additional steps and activities suggested in the relationship of Moses and Joshua:

- Formally establish the relationship at the proper time. "Then he laid his hands on him and commissioned him, just as the Lord had spoken through Moses" (Numbers 27:23).
- Start early with the opportunity for training. Numbers 11:28 gives the following description: "Joshua the son of Nun, the attendant of Moses from his youth."
- Take your understudy with you so that he or she can observe and learn. "So Moses arose with Joshua his servant, and Moses went up to the mountain of God" (Exodus 24:13).
- Provide time for private consultation. "Thus the Lord used to speak to Moses face to face, just as a man speaks to his friend. When Moses returned to the camp, his servant Joshua, the son of Nun, a young man, would not depart from the tent" (Exodus 33:11).
- Correct your understudy in an appropriate but direct way when he or she needs correction. Joshua asked Moses to restrain two men who were prophesying in the camp. Moses responded, "Are you jealous for my sake? Would that all the Lord's people were prophets, that the Lord would put His Spirit upon them!" (Numbers 11:29).
- Formally introduce the future leader at the proper time. In a special ceremony in the sight of all Israel, Moses encouraged and challenged his replacement.

He went on to point Joshua to the Lord, not to himself. In addition, Moses re-assured Joshua of God's protection and faithfulness (Deuteronomy 31:7–8).

‣ Have some ideas already? Whether you're interviewing a new teacher, con-ducting a difficult conference with unhappy parents, preparing for a board meeting, or observing a teacher and developing a meaningful write-up—wherever you go and whatever you're doing—be on the lookout for informa-tion to put in the ears of the future leaders that God has called you to develop.

Personalized Leadership

In *Mastering Church Management* (1990, 141), Don Cousins describes the need for working with each person as an individual, citing Ken Blanchard's writing about training leaders. Cousins endorses Blanchard's model called "situ-ational leadership" (Blanchard, Zigarmi, and Zigarmi 1985), but he prefers to rename it "personalized leadership" because Cousins says that he wants to keep his focus on leading people, not just handling situations (1990, 141). He uses Blanchard's model to outline four critical steps in developing leaders:

Direction stage. The first stage involves the careful training of the inexperienced mentee. Basically, the leader is actually doing the ministry through the trainee (Cousins 1990, 141). This process can take the form of regular meetings to dis-cuss step-by-step activities, the teacher's demonstration of necessary steps, or the side-by-side execution of the tasks. The extent of the supervision depends on variables such as the level of maturity and experience the mentee brings to the relationship, the critical nature of the projects that need to be completed, and the length of time the student requires to gain confidence and skill in the new area of training (Cousins 1990; Blanchard, Zigarmi, and Zigarmi 1985).

Coaching stage. The next step takes place when the mentee's confidence and com-petence grow. At this point, the leader steps off the court and begins to observe the performance, making specific corrections as necessary. The student makes suggestions, and the two work together; the project is a joint venture. The coach's primary responsibilities are affirmation and redirection (Cousins 1990, 141–42).

Support stage. The first two steps may take as much as a year each, depending on the progress of the follower and the sophistication of the new task. At this point, he or she is ready for the third step in the relationship. A significant milestone takes place as the leader turns over more responsibility to the follower, who begins to set the agenda and prioritize what needs to be done. The mentee knows what must be accomplished and primarily needs to know that the mentor is there to provide emotional support, encouragement, affirmation, and, if necessary, correction. The coach now becomes a cheerleader (Cousins 1990, 142).

Delegation stage. The final step is to turn over the project or the activity to the new leader. Even though reporting continues and the mentor maintains his or her interest in the mentee, the task now belongs to the latter. Unfortunately, the act of turning over a ministry or a responsibility all too often happens first before any guiding and training take place (Cousins 1990, 142). The usual result, in this case, is a "train wreck" that brings about the dismissal of an employee who began with great enthusiasm for the task but who received no training or guidance. Another difficulty can occur at this point. The mentor can be unwilling to let go of the activity for which the follower was trained, and the mentor can insist on continuing to micromanage the project and the trainee. This micromanagement can result in the younger person's not feeling trusted or adequate to do the job and may mean that, though well trained, the new leader will leave the organization in pursuit of a yard of his or her own to cut and tend.

THE LEADERSHIP DEVELOPMENT OF ADMIRAL LORD NELSON

We can clearly see Blanchard's four-step process to develop new leaders in the leadership development of England's greatest naval hero: Admiral Lord Nelson. Had Nelson joined a sailing ship bound for battle during wartime, he would have been thrust into a dangerous and bewildering world. He would perhaps have sailed immediately, and he would have found himself in a terrifying naval action within weeks, before he could understand how to work, or even live, in the "wooden world." In an age when systematic training of naval officers did not commonly take place, Nelson had a progressive education as a seaman and as an officer. Note below how this admiral's experience compares to Blanchard's model:

Direction stage. Although little formal instruction of seamen and officers took place, except what the ship's officers might provide in their spare time,

Nelson's uncle secured a place on a ship where Nelson would learn to raise the anchors, keep a lookout, help operate the guns, and climb the rigging in a storm to take in sail. At that time, "there was a small Naval Academy at Portsmouth, but most people in the know regarded it as a waste of time. It certainly did not warrant missing the chance to serve under a captain who was also one's uncle" (Lavery 2003, 15).

Coaching stage. Later Nelson would learn the extra skills an officer needed—the technical ones of navigation, seamanship, gunnery, naval tactics, and management and leadership of men. His uncle encouraged him to learn navigation, holding out the reward that if he did so he would progress to the boats that the ship carried, the longboat and the cutter. Nelson became a midshipman after fourteen months, and he was given authority over some of the crew, including command of 8 to 12 men "who would handle the boat under oars or sail, ferrying officers and crew to and from the shore" (Lavery 2003, 17). Nelson would later reflect on the experiences: "Thus by degrees I became a good pilot, for vessels of that description, from Chatham to the Tower of London, down the Swin, and the North Foreland; and confident of myself among rocks and sands, which has many times been of great comfort to me" (18).

Support stage. On April 14, 1777, Nelson wrote one of his many letters that have survived. It was written to his brother, and in that letter, Nelson announced that he had passed the lieutenant's examination five days earlier. His first appointment as a commissioned officer was under a friend of his uncle's on the ship *Lowestoffe.* This ship took him on his second trip to the Caribbean Islands. During this voyage the *Lowestoffe* captured a smaller schooner, and the captain decided to have it accompany his ship. He gave Nelson command of the schooner. "It was not the same as the independent command of a ship, which is what Nelson most desired, but it was more than a ship's boat and it aided Nelson's development in more ways than one." Later Nelson would write, "In this vessel I made myself a complete pilot for all the passages through the (Keys) Islands" (Lavery 2003, 22–24).

Delegation stage. On June 11, 1779, the opportunity that Nelson had longed for came: promotion to captain of the twenty-eight-gun *Hinchinbrook,* a small frigate recently captured from a French fleet. At the early age of twenty, Nelson served as a full captain in the Royal Navy. He held the lives of 200 men in his hands (Lavery 2003, 27–28).

In time Nelson would rise through the ranks and become a rear admiral. As the captain of the flagship the HMS *Victory*, Nelson led the British fleet against the French in what would prove to be a major turning point in the Napoleonic War. Before the Battle of Trafalgar, his signal officer issued this inspirational exhortation from Nelson to the rest of the fleet: "England expects that every man will do his duty" (Lavery 2003, 130). Indeed Lord Nelson did, dying aboard the *Victory* from a sniper's bullet (Lavery 2003).

Two Minutes That Build Confidence and Trust

The vital importance of instructional leadership on the part of the administrator is well established in the literature over the last twenty years (Coley 2006; Brown 2007–2008; Sergiovanni 1995). An integral part of this leadership is regular dialogue and interaction with teachers about what is occurring in their classrooms. Of course this conversation is severely limited if the administrator has infrequent contact with the staff during actual teaching moments. This being said, it is my experience that all too often classroom observations are not taking place regularly and that the resulting feedback is often not very beneficial during the sporadic moments when they do occur. At the core of this situation is a disheartening but very correctable truth—many administrators, especially inexperienced ones, do not go into classrooms because they simply do not know what to look for or how to make meaningful comments about what they observe.

The veracity and significance of observing classroom instruction is echoed by Gordon Brown, one of the leading clinicians in the field of education and specifically in instructional supervision. He asks two questions that are on the minds of many administrators: "How frequently should supervisors observe classes?" and "Is there an optimum number of visits for ensuring that instructional improvement will take place?" (2007–2008, 23). Though research does not give exact answers, we can say that the amount of time that principals spend in observing classes is one of the three most important predictors of student achievement (Heck 1992).

This lack of personal confidence on the part of a leader may lead to a lack of trust between the leader and a teacher. A teacher may ask the questions, If my principal never visits my room, how does she know what's really going on day to day? and How do I know she will adequately support me if an issue with a parent were to arise? Tragically, this breakdown of confidence and trust can feed off itself and lead to misunderstandings and further distrust.

The research of Carolyn Downey, an educator and a researcher who has spent more than forty years examining this concept, espouses short, frequent classroom visits. Downey and her coauthors state, "If our goal is one of professional growth rather than evaluation of the individual, a short visit is all that is required to provide ample data to promote teacher growth. With a longer stay, too much data are collected. In fact, it is our opinion that we tend to make more judgments when staying in classrooms for longer periods of time. The short observation allows you to frequent all the classrooms on a regular basis rather than see just a few a month. The principal will have a more accurate picture of what is going on in the school when he or she is able to visit all of the classrooms regularly" (2004, 3). Let's consider a well-known football analogy as we begin our plans to make these supervisory principles a reality in your school.

Every football team, from Pop Warner to the NFL, has a plan for a "two-minute drill." The coach and his players prepare for the last two minutes of the game when time is running out and the team has to score points to win. As a part of the team's preparation, the coaches and offensive players script a special set of plays they plan to use. They focus on a limited number of plays and develop these for a very special purpose—to go down the field as quickly as possible, using the team's strengths.

If you are a football fan, perhaps you have already jumped ahead to connecting the necessity of preparing for this drill in a football game and the great advantage an instructional leader can gain if he or she has planned for a two-minute drill in a brief classroom observation. Let's review the similarities:
+ A limited amount of time
+ A scripted plan or approach
+ A specific focus
+ An execution that leads to success

How many classrooms do you have on one hallway? Six? Twelve? You schedule thirty minutes starting at ten o'clock, during which you visit every classroom for about two minutes. During that time you jot down a few words or phrases about what you are observing.

Wait a minute, you say, how much can I actually grasp about what's going on in such a short time? Let's begin designing our game plan by establishing four categories: teacher, content, student, and environment. As you consider each category, list in each only those things that *may* be present during a brief observation in a classroom. You may not observe all the items in each category during every visit, but we are focusing on important instructional components you can observe and comment on in a meaningful way even though you will be present for just a snapshot of the lesson. Omit from this list any educational concept or activity that takes more than about two minutes to observe and evaluate accurately. For example, a teacher's overall performance must reflect the ability to develop a sequential lesson plan, but clearly you cannot comment on that ability when you stop by for a brief stay. Every teacher also needs to respond to individual student needs, but you may not always have the ability to see this characteristic of effective teaching during a two-minute visit. Review the items in figure 7.1 and evaluate the possibility of making a meaningful comment about one or more of the items under each category:

Teacher	Content	Student	Environment
⬦ Positive interaction	⬦ Lesson objective on the board	⬦ On task	⬦ Safe
⬦ "With-itness"	⬦ Consistency with school's curriculum	⬦ Cooperative	⬦ Orderly
⬦ Preparation	⬦ Assignments/ Homework posted	⬦ Attentive	⬦ Appropriate seating arrangement

Fig. 7.1

Downey and her coauthors have developed a five-step walk-through observation structure that is similar to the quadrants. The structure they have devised, intended for two-to-three-minute visits to classrooms, consists of the following (2004, 21):

1. Student orientation to the work
2. Curricular decision points
3. Instructional decision points

4. "Walk-the-Walls," looking for evidence, such as projects or portfolios, showing past objectives taught or instructional decisions used to teach the objectives that are present in the classroom

5. Safety and health issues

After a two-to-three-minute visit in a middle-school teacher's room, your note back to the teacher might read like this: "I enjoyed dropping by this morning. Your room arrangement was excellent for the cooperative-learning activity you designed. Your students were really involved! The lesson objective you had posted is very important for this age group. Keep up the good work."

The write-up following a visit to a fourth-grade class might say this: "Hearing your students pray this morning really started my day off in a special way. Your room is such a good atmosphere for learning. It really helps the students who have been absent to see the assignments posted on the side board. I look forward to another visit soon."

How do you think most teachers would respond if they received one of these notes in their boxes? Do you agree that such a communication would build a teacher's confidence and trust? Once again, Downey and her coauthors' comments reflect agreement: "The major goal of this brief informal observation is to trigger a thought that might be useful for the teacher to consider, one that might help the teacher in his or her decision making about effective practice.... When we provide follow-up, it is to give opportunities for reflective thought" (2004, 3).

Although you can use such notes effectively, please note that Downey and her coauthors argue that a better approach to providing feedback is to dialogue with the teacher: "The note is a one-way communication. It seldom provides dialogue except when a teacher feels compelled to come and speak to you about it. *Two-way interactions* help clarify ideas, influence thought, and allow you to see the teacher's reaction to your ideas. A note seldom stretches a person's cognitive field. It is about something already accomplished. It feels good for a short while, but it is merely an event; it comes from the top down, and then it is over. Our goal is to continue reflective inquiry about a teacher's practice over time" (Downey et al. 2004, 48; italics in original).

Another important concept in the preparation stage of this process is to discuss with your staff, as a whole or by department, the points of emphasis they believe are important for the benefit of their students and for their own professional development. Perhaps you can suggest some, such as writing lesson objectives on the board and posting each evening's assignment. Again, such communication between you and the teachers builds trust and understanding, and the entire process leads to achieving both better instruction and important student outcomes.

Now, back to that hallway. I predicted you never dreamed you could visit every room in less than one class period and give the teachers a brief write-up that will send them home smiling. How about stopping by at least once every other week? By the time parent conferences are scheduled, you will have plenty of firsthand observations; and when you schedule a formal observation with each teacher before Thanksgiving, your presence will not distract the students. The teachers will be more relaxed, and they will even look forward to receiving your feedback. Let's break the huddle—you're ready for a two-minute drill!

FIFTEEN MINUTES THAT PROVIDE ENCOURAGEMENT

Administrators, lead teachers, and department heads have an often-untapped source of enormous power: the opportunity to communicate insights about successful teaching moments to their colleagues. And it takes fifteen minutes, or even less time.

In the previous discussion, "Two Minutes That Build Confidence and Trust," I described a process of interaction called an administrator's two-minute drill, which allows an instructional leader to make valuable connections with teachers while staying in each room about two or three minutes. In that section, I referenced the research of Carolyn Downey and her associates (2004), who recommend "the three-minute classroom walk-through." Educator Sally J. Zepeda, a professor of educational administration at the University of Georgia, differs slightly with the approaches presented there: "Although that method will certainly get supervision out of the main office, the principal is encouraged to spend more than three to five minutes in the classroom during an informal observation to have a meaningful experience. The egg-timer approach to classroom observation of this duration is a 'blitz' in which the observation's brevity minimizes data collection. It would be preferable to conduct fewer but longer informal observations on a daily basis to connect with teachers and to derive a more accurate sense of the classroom activities observed" (2005, 19).

I wish to enthusiastically endorse the two-minute drill and now introduce the concept that Zepeda proposes: informal visits of fifteen minutes. Both are useful, and both are necessary. As I introduce you to this second model, consider which style of informal observations will yield the best results in your unique school.

Gordon Brown (2007–2008) and Thomas Sergiovanni (1995) write about the value of informal visits as part of the overall responsibility of administrators to monitor and evaluate professional performance in the classroom. This chapter presents a systematic method of collecting valuable snapshots of your instructional program and of your teachers' pedagogical skills. No one would argue that brief, unplanned visits should replace well-designed, formal evaluations associated with clinical supervision (Coley 2006; Brown 2007–2008), especially as administrators prepare for summative evaluation conferences. However, all too often administrators miss out on the value of spending fifteen minutes in a classroom and watching a colleague interact with students. This fifteen-minute approach can provide you with information about the following:

+ Identification of areas for improvement
+ Update on activities in classrooms
+ Curriculum evaluation
+ Facilities evaluation
+ Observation of instructional techniques
+ Insights into student performance and behavior
+ Insights into class chemistry
+ New ideas to share with your faculty about best practices
+ New ideas to pursue in future faculty development sessions

In addition to providing needed encouragement to the teacher, the fifteen-minute informal visits may very well encourage and energize you as you see the school's philosophy and mission take hold. Oddly enough, another positive benefit is stress reduction for the busy administrator. In the article "Walk-Throughs Are on the Move" in *Education World*, the editor in chief, Gary

Hopkins, states the following: "School leaders are under a lot of stress—but if exercise is a stress antidote, then principals might be among the healthiest managers around. That's because a lot of principals are doing an awful lot of walking. They're using a technique known as the *walk-through* to take the pulse of student learning in their schools" (2009; italics in original).

If informal observations yield such powerful results and if administrators can so effectively manage these observations, why aren't more administrators using this approach? As I noted previously, many administrators may very well be thinking, "But I don't know enough to make valuable, meaningful remarks without a lot of preparation." Perhaps this belief, more than the paucity of time, is the most significant de-motivator.

To further help you feel prepared, study the items listed in figure 7.2. I encourage you to view the list under each category not as a checklist but as a list of potential concepts and activities that you may observe during a fifteen-minute session in a classroom.

Environment
+ Orderly
+ Attractive
+ Informative: lesson objective posted
+ Comfortable
+ Conducive
+ Helpful: assignments posted

Student Participation
+ Engaged
+ Active
+ Respectful
+ Involved in cooperative learning
+ Capable of working independently
+ Self-managed

Areas for Reflection
+ A noticeable weakness in one of the other categories
+ A department or schoolwide point of emphasis that is lacking

Content
+ Biblical integration
+ A set curriculum that is followed
+ Valuable information
+ Challenging material
+ Clear objective
+ Meaningful assignments

Teacher Characteristics and Instructional Techniques
+ Proximity to students
+ Eye contact
+ Voice
+ Body and hand movements
+ Pace of lesson
+ Type of instruction
+ Response to discipleship issues
+ Interaction with students
+ Godly role model

Fig. 7.2

Leading Change
Managing Without Mutiny

The one skill the leader must possess to make his or her vision a reality

◆ Lessons from Britain's Royal Navy

◆ John Kotter and Nehemiah on change management

By definition, leadership focuses on tomorrow and a preferable future (Barna 1992), and this focus requires leaders to employ skills related to change management. Without such skills an organization will perpetually remain the same, or it will devolve into mutiny and chaos as groups or individuals in the organization do one of two things—demand change in a way that undermines the organization or resist change with all their might. Once again our nautical metaphor gives us a powerful perspective as we reflect on naval stories and compare those events with the all-too-numerous narratives we have heard regarding the horrible loss of harmony in a Christian school community when the leaders do not respond to their followers' need for change or when a new administrator begins to take aim at established ways of "doing school."

Mutiny in Britain's Royal Navy

Richard O'Neill, a writer and an editor who has specialized in military history for over forty years, writes, "The crew of any ship was a small floating community. It was a society with its own hierarchy, laws, customs, and professional language…. The social welfare and the good behavior of the crew in the ships of the Royal Navy was the responsibility of the ship's officers. The captain himself was responsible for the conduct of the officers under his command. All of this was regulated by the Articles of War … and various sets of regulations and instructions that existed to underpin the lawful authority of the captain. It could be argued, therefore, that the navy's worst crimes, mutiny and desertion, were largely the fault of bad officers" (2003, 140).

Three famous mutinies from British naval history provide modern leaders with valuable insights and severe warnings. High inflation in the last half of the eighteenth century severely lowered the value of the British sailors' pay (Hill 1987). In addition, a new wartime impressment system meant that there were large numbers of inexperienced recruits who did not mix well with the career seamen (Miller, Vandome, and McBrewster 2009). During the mutiny at Spithead in 1797, the sailors protested their working conditions and demanded a pay raise, which would have been the first in over a century. A small amount of violence broke out after the mutineers' elected delegates tried to deal with the Royal Navy. However, the situation was calmed successfully, and Admiral Lord

Howe negotiated an agreement. The crews obtained better working conditions and a pay raise. Because the sailors handled themselves in a relatively peaceful way, they received no reprisals (Moore 1999b).

Unfortunately, the response to another 1797 rebellion against change and outrageous working conditions did not end as amicably at the Nore as it did at Spithead. The discontented sailors at the Nore made numerous demands, such as ending impressments, poor-quality rations, and unequal pay. They also demanded a change in leave entitlements. Their mutiny intensified with a blockade of London and even more grandiose demands including modification of the Articles of War. But there was dissent among the sailors serving as delegates. Because the unification of the mutineers broke down and the Royal Navy denied the ships food and water, the mutiny failed. Several of the leading mutineers were briefly tried for treason and piracy and were hanged, and other key offenders were either flogged or imprisoned (Moore 1999a, 1999c).

Whether an organization experiences change from the bottom up or from the top down, the leadership must manage the change well. Spithead gives us an example in which the change management came a bit late and as a result of a mutiny, but nevertheless succeeded. The Nore teaches us that discontented crew members who feel they have no voice can break out into riotous mutiny that has devastating results. Could more effective leadership have prevented the Nore mutiny or settled it peacefully? We don't know, but we can, at any rate, agree that leadership by oppression never works and certainly cannot effectively usher in change.

The most famous mutiny in the history of the Royal Navy occurred on the frigate *Hermione*, which would become known as the "Black Ship." Captain Hugh Pigot enforced many outrageous brutalities such as flogging the last man down from the mast in a show of force to encourage all crew members to be brisk about their duties. "On one occasion, three seamen, anxious not to be the last down from aloft under threat of punishment for being last man down, lost their footing and fell to the deck. Pigot ordered the dead bodies to be thrown overboard without the least ceremony." This act by Pigot proved to be the breaking point for the disheartened crew. In September 1797 the crew mutinied in the West Indies, killing all the officers, and handed the boat over to the Spanish. O'Neill summarizes these events in the book *Patrick O'Brian's Navy*. He draws this conclusion about leadership on ships at that time: "The greatest enemy to everyone on board was the sea itself and survival depended on teamwork, discipline, and skill. An individual sailor might desert his ship or commit an act deemed mutinous, but when a large part of a crew acted together to commit either mutiny or desertion, it was the sign of a badly officered ship. Oppression and tyranny in an officer might indicate an unbalanced mind, or simply a cruel nature, but more often extreme severity was usually a cloak for poor leadership and skill" (2003, 141).

HELMSMAN'S LOG

A few years ago I was called to assist a fifteen-year-old school that was close to crashing on the rocks and closing in the middle of the summer. The board of directors described declining enrollment and shaky finances and the sudden departure of the administrator but made no mention of the faculty. During my first two visits to the community I sought out some of the teachers in an effort to solicit their perspective on the health of the school. After my many years of experience, what I heard that summer still shocks me. In his effort to institute significant changes, the recently departed administrator had emotionally isolated most of the faculty from any feeling of unity or community spirit. He discouraged disagreements and even professional discussion and met both with threats of retribution. Several teachers were told directly that for them to even speak with the board about the administrator's decisions or style would mean immediate dismissal. I saw a collection of individuals who appeared to be Christlike, submissive, and professionally capable in every way but who had become totally dispirited, cowed, and disheartened. Giving the former school leader the benefit of the doubt, whether it was deserved or not, I can say without question that this young school had growing pains and needed a fresh vision. But how the administrator went about

Helmsman's Log

trying to achieve needed changes nearly broke the spirit of the faculty. I repeat O'Neill's conclusion: *"Oppression and tyranny in an officer might indicate an unbalanced mind, or simply a cruel nature, but more often extreme severity was usually a cloak for poor leadership and skill"* (2003, 141; italics mine). ⚓

Change Management According to John Kotter and Nehemiah

One of the prominent names in change management today is John Kotter, the author of numerous books including *Leading Change* and the coauthor of *Our Iceberg Is Melting: Changing and Succeeding Under Any Conditions*. Kotter developed an eight-step process for successful change. Research and business experience led Kotter to conclude that "90 percent of organizations were either ignoring relevant changes or were trying to adjust in ways that were not meeting their aspirations. Too much time and money was being spent to achieve too little, with too much pain and frustration all around." Kotter also concluded that "dealing with change was becoming an increasingly important skill for people not only at the top of organizations, but up and down hierarchies." For organizational change to be successful, nearly everyone in the organization must play an important role in helping the organization adapt. "Yet in the vast majority of the organizations [Kotter] studied, most people didn't know what to do, felt threatened, or were convinced top management didn't want their help" (Kotter and Rathgeber 2005, 139–41). I will briefly review Kotter's eight steps, using biblical reflections based on Nehemiah, a book of the Bible about an Old Testament leader who both responded to a need for change and led one of the most miraculous change efforts in the history of humankind.

Set the Stage

1. *Create a sense of urgency.* "Help others see the need for change and the importance of acting immediately" (Kotter and Rathgeber 2005, 130). Nehemiah heard the following from his brother Hanani and some men from Judah concerning the

Jews in Jerusalem: "The remnant there in the province who survived the captivity are in great distress and reproach, and the wall of Jerusalem is broken down and its gates are burned with fire" (Nehemiah 1:3). The absence of a protecting wall in their culture is difficult for us to appreciate. It was spiritually important because Jerusalem was supposed to represent God to the surrounding nations, and the dilapidated condition of the city was a painful embarrassment. Also, the broken-down wall left the city constantly vulnerable to thieves and wild animals. Perhaps we can picture trying to protect a home and our belongings in the Wild West without a fence or other means of protection.

Nehemiah traveled to Jerusalem and after a few days met with city leaders. He said, "You see the bad situation we are in, that Jerusalem is desolate and its gates burned by fire. Come, let us rebuild the wall of Jerusalem so that we will no longer be a reproach" (Nehemiah 2:17).

2. *Pull together the guiding team.* "Make sure there is a powerful group guiding the change—one with leadership skills, credibility, communications ability, authority, analytical skills, and a sense of urgency" (Kotter and Rathgeber 2005, 130). In addition to the leaders mentioned in Nehemiah 2:16—the Jews, the priests, the nobles, and the officials—there is a lengthy and impressive list of leaders in Nehemiah 3:

* Eliashib, the high priest (v. 1)
* Rephaiah, the official of half the district of Jerusalem (v. 9)
* Shallum, the official of half the district of Jerusalem (v. 12)
* Malchijah, the official of the district of Beth-haccerem (v. 14)
* Shallum, the official of the district of Mizpah (v. 15)
* Nehemiah, the official of half the district of Beth-zur (v. 16)
* The Levites (v. 17)
* Hashabiah, the official of half the district of Keilah (v. 17)
* Bavvai, the official of the other half of Keilah (v. 18)
* Ezer, the official of Mizpah (v. 19)

This represents an impressive "buy in" for Nehemiah, especially since he was the new guy in town. As we study Nehemiah 3, we see that these officials brought along family and associates to participate in the arduous work of rebuilding a dilapidated stone wall.

Decide What to Do

3. *Develop the change vision and strategy.* "Clarify how the future will be different from the past, and how you can make that future a reality" (Kotter and Rathgeber 2005, 130). Nehemiah's plan for reconstruction makes for an interesting study in the motivation of employees or of community members. As you reread Nehemiah 3, notice the occurrence of phrases related to repairs on the wall in sections located near the workers' own homes:

+ "repairs opposite his house" (v. 10)
+ "repairs for his district" (v. 17)
+ "repairs in front of their house" (v. 23)
+ "repairs beside his house" (v. 23)
+ "repairs, each in front of his house" (v. 28)
+ "repairs in front of his house" (v. 29)

And there were probably assignments made throughout Nehemiah 3 that don't reflect the connection that existed between the worker and the part of the wall he was called to repair.

Make It Happen

4. *Communicate for understanding and buy in.* "Make sure as many others as possible understand and accept the vision and the strategy" (Kotter and Rathgeber 2005, 131). Nehemiah and his co-laborers experienced intense opposition from other Jewish and some non-Jewish leaders who tried desperately to paint the reconstruction of the wall as a precursor to rebellion against the Persian Empire. Nehemiah 2:19 reads, "What is this thing you are doing? Are you rebelling against the king?" and the ridicule intensified in 4:1–3. Tobiah the Ammonite uttered his famous insult: "Even what they are building—if a fox should jump on it, he would break their stone wall down!" (4:3). It was further reported to Nehemiah that the enemies said, "They will not know or see until we come among them, kill them and put a stop to the work" (4:11). The Jews who lived near the enemies told Nehemiah and his followers ten times, "They will come up against us from every place where you may turn" (4:12).

Nehemiah responded to the extraordinary pressure from the enemies by calling on the Lord: "We prayed to our God, and because of them we set up a guard against them day and night" (4:9). And he communicated with his followers, boldly encouraging them and reminding them of a reason to fight: "When I saw their fear, I rose and spoke to the nobles, the officials and the rest of the people: 'Do not be afraid of them; remember the Lord who is great and awesome, and fight for your brothers, your sons, your daughters, your wives and your houses'" (4:14).

HELMSMAN'S LOG

Read the following excerpt from my interview with Eugene J. Gabrell on March 1, 2008. As an experienced sailor, he recounts his time as a young student in the Coast Guard:

As a fourth-class cadet (freshman) in the summer of 1975 at the United States Coast Guard Academy located in New London, Connecticut, I had the experience of sailing on the USCGC *Eagle*, a 30,000-square-foot-sail-area Barkentine training ship. At night we would string hammocks below decks for sleeping. We would keep in mind that under sail the *Eagle* would constantly list to one side or the other. The result of this would be a 1-foot step on one side of our sleeping hammock and a 3-foot step on the other side. At reveille the following morning, we would try to remember to de-bunk on the short side of the hammock. However, during some nights the ship would change tacks while we slept, thus reversing the high and low sides of the hammock. When this happened, the following morning at reveille we would find ourselves losing our footing and crashing on the deck or into the bulkheads. This event was always a comical sight for the more experienced upperclassmen.

Reflect on changes at your school and the preparedness of the faculty. Are there inexperienced crew members who have tripped and fallen because of unexpected changes? ⚓

5. *Empower others to act.* "Remove as many barriers as possible so that those who want to make the vision a reality can do so" (Kotter and Rathgeber 2005, 131). Nehemiah continued with a make-it-happen spirit, giving reminders of God's protection and making specific plans for his men to do their part. He "stationed men in the lowest parts of the space behind the wall, the exposed places, and [he] stationed the people in families with their swords, spears and bows" (4:13). In addition, he empowered each crew member to concentrate on his task. "From that day on, half of my servants carried on the work while half of them held the spears, the shields, the bows and the breastplates; and the captains were behind the whole house of Judah" (4:16).

6. *Produce short-term wins.* "Create some visible, unambiguous successes as soon as possible" (Kotter and Rathgeber 2005, 131). In the midst of these struggles and the discouragements, one verse jumps out as a short-term win for this odd collection of construction workers: "So we built the wall and the whole wall was joined together to half its height, for the people had a mind to work" (4:6). Having many options for how to approach the project, Nehemiah directed the laborers to work at all sections of the wall at once and then to join the sections together. It's not difficult to imagine that even at half the projected height, the workers were able to get a sense of accomplishment as they saw the wall take shape.

7. *Don't let up.* "Press harder and faster after the first successes. Be relentless with initiating change after change until the vision is a reality" (Kotter and Rathgeber 2005, 131). Nehemiah encouraged the workers as they tirelessly worked with one hand and held a weapon with the other (4:17). Regarding any attack that might occur as they continued to work, he told them, "Our God will fight for us" (4:20). Nehemiah further challenged them to pull 24-7 shifts of duty! "So we carried on the work with half of them holding spears from dawn until the stars appeared. At that time I also said to the people, 'Let each man with his servant spend the night within Jerusalem so that they may be a guard for us by night and a laborer by day'" (4:21–22).

Make It Stick

8. *Create a new culture.* "Hold on to the new ways of behaving, and make sure they succeed, until they become strong enough to replace old traditions" (Kotter and Rathgeber 2005, 131). In just fifty-two days (6:15), Nehemiah and his

followers restored the wall surrounding Jerusalem—a miracle in some people's minds on the order of parting the Red Sea or the Jordan River. Modern readers must consider carefully what took place here: building a wall about two and a half miles in circumference and ten feet across without the modern power tools and massive cranes we take for granted. Just imagine the human energy and teamwork necessary to move a granite block just a few feet using basic machines such as a lever, a wheel, or a pulley.

And at the conclusion of this miracle, the people came together in worship under the leadership of Nehemiah, their governor and general contractor; Ezra, the high priest; and the Levites. In a short, powerful description, Nehemiah 8:1 tells us that "all the people gathered as one man." We should long for such harmony in our ministries. Following a time of worship focused on the reading of God's Word, which was heard for the first time by most of those gathered there in Jerusalem, Nehemiah urged the crowd to disperse and go home for feasting and celebrating. This event illustrates a powerful tool available to all leaders but frequently underused—developing and cementing cultural change by seizing the moments of victory and urging the participants to enjoy the accomplishments.

What's Different in a Godly Leader?

As we have already observed, Nehemiah's leadership qualities and behaviors are examples of the concepts we find in the current discussions in the literature on change management. However, Nehemiah's model includes dimensions and steps that we either don't see or don't see as clearly in Kotter's leading-change process.

First, from the beginning of the narrative, the reader of Nehemiah sees that a godly leader is a *person of prayer*—an absolutely essential ingredient for the leadership of your school. "In Nehemiah 1, Nehemiah receives word that Jerusalem's walls are in shambles. The stones are in ruins, and the gates have been consumed by fire. God's people are disgraced as they live among the rubble and fall victim to passing caravans of thieves and looters" (Coley 2006, 94). Right away, Nehemiah demonstrated the behavior of godly leaders who earnestly turn to the Lord. As we did in chapter 3, let's consider his words: "When I heard these words, I sat down and wept and mourned for days; and I was fasting and praying before the God of heaven" (1:4). He was a "leader—

from the knees up!" (Swindoll 1978, 30). Yes, leaders must certainly declare the urgency of the need for change, but they must not move forward or speak without the Lord's confirmation.

Second, Nehemiah's model includes the significant step of both *thorough research about the present realities and insights about the past realities*. In a quotation previously referred to in our discussion of a school's vision statement, George Barna succinctly explains these connections as he describes the formulation of a vision as "foresight with insight based on hindsight" (1992, 28). Nehemiah 2 carefully explains the quiet tour that Nehemiah took of the city "he had been taught to revere but had never visited. After a late-night tour of the perimeter to examine the full extent of the damage and the work that lay ahead, he was prepared to meet with the city's leaders" (Coley 2006, 95). For this new leader it was only a matter of days. For new school leaders it could be a matter of months or even years. In a chapter titled "Navigating the Maze: Coping with Constant Change," Jerry Haddock, director of the ACSI Southern California Region, powerfully points out that change must start with people, not with an organization:

> Administrators should make a careful study of the school before initiating major changes. This process requires analyzing the entire school culture by getting to know the people and finding out as much as possible about them. Administrators should also determine the current level of support. What has the school been through? Did previous leaders promise more than they could deliver? These are important questions to ask before charging in with an agenda that the school community may not be ready to accept. Before making significant changes, leaders new to their positions should know their school, know its history, know its strengths, know the areas of vulnerability, know the hurts, and know the disappointments. (2002, 279; italics in original)

As the new vision or projected changes develop, leaders, third, must *help each member of the community identify a significant way in which he or she can connect to the new structure or approach*. In Nehemiah 3 the construction foreman chose to assign to each construction crew the wall section that was closest to the crew members' homes and neighbors. He knew that the leaders and their inexperienced laborers would be highly motivated to tackle the arduous tasks before them because these builders would hope to do the work well and quickly before the next invaders showed up at their doors. Over the years, it has been my observation that leaders and their change managers could lessen or eliminate much of the conflict that arises during a season of change if they would actively connect the lives of the people who have invested in the ministries to concrete, significant parts of the new vision.

Effective change-management leaders need a fourth quality that is more powerfully portrayed in the book of Nehemiah than in Kotter's literature—a commitment to *focus on the needs of individuals* even when the leaders could see the individuals' needs as a distraction from focusing on new goals. In Nehemiah 4 the Jews reported their dread of attack by those who opposed the wall's construction. Nehemiah posted guards around the two and a half miles of the construction project. In Nehemiah 5, there was "a great outcry" (v. 1) because some Jews could not feed their families in time of famine and some had to mortgage their land and homes to survive and pay the king's tax. In some cases, Jews were forcing the children of other Jews into bondage because of the economic crisis. This compassionate leader diverted his energies from the wall in order to solve these conflicts.

Christian leaders reflect a fifth quality of Nehemiah's model when they *point their people to the Lord and His blessing as those people celebrate victories.* While Kotter does trumpet the value of celebrations, we must be quick to make a distinction between celebrating human efforts and celebrating the energy, power, direction, and success that God provides. Nehemiah directed this group of successful builders to focus on God and His blessings on the community (8:10). It is interesting to note both that Nehemiah, Ezra, and the Levites encouraged their people not to grieve in response to Ezra's reading of the Word and that Nehemiah declared a day of rejoicing at what the Lord had done. That might be missing in your home, your school, your community of believers—a great day of rejoicing!

Solidifying change (point eight: "Create a new culture," under the subhead "Make It Stick") can also take place as Christian leaders demonstrate *leadership by outrage,*[*] as Nehemiah 13 illustrates. Thomas Sergiovanni has argued that leaders must protect the core values of their communities by passionately objecting to violations of the established covenants:

> Leadership by outrage is a symbolic act that communicates importance and meaning and that touches people in ways not possible when leadership is viewed

---

*For further discussion of this concept, see pages 122–25 of *The Helmsman: Leading with Courage and Wisdom* (Coley 2006).

only as something objective and calculated. Leaders use outrage to highlight issues of purpose defined by the school's shared covenant, and this outrage adds considerable value to their leadership practice.

... They are outraged when they see these values ignored or violated. The values of the common core represent nonnegotiables that comprise cultural strands that define a way of life in the school. (1995, 138)

I once attended a high-school softball game as a spectator and observed leadership by outrage acted out in a powerful way. Early in the game, the home team's lineup was struggling to get a hit because of the speed of the pitches that the visiting pitcher had thrown. Perhaps to upset this pitcher or maybe just for entertainment, a college-age spectator yelled an insult at her during a quiet lull in the action. No one laughed, and the crowd froze.

Before anyone could move or react, the batter who was standing in the on-deck circle and was no more than fifteen feet from her home crowd, turned sternly and spoke without hesitation: "Do not say anything else like that!" Moments later her teammate who had just struck out was passing the fence where the crowd sat. That teammate likewise showed her outrage by saying, "Don't say anything else!" That night I observed two student leaders who demonstrated with boldness their commitment to Christlike values and unflinchingly expressed their outrage.

Walking the Plank
Dismissing Without a Big Splash

The three most critical moments the leader faces in the storm

+ Splash #1: dismissing a faculty member
+ Splash #2: disciplining a student
+ Splash #3: being dismissed yourself

One of the most sinister phrases associated with the villainy of pirates is *walk the plank*. We have all seen movies or read books depicting the terrible act by pirates—they force a helpless man or woman, usually bound and blindfolded, to walk onto a wobbly piece of wood extended from a ship. Then at least one pirate prods the victim with a sword until there is no more plank, and then the victim falls into a sea of hungry predators.

The reality of this scene is extremely difficult to gauge because there exists little evidence that it ever took place. This lack of evidence should not come as a surprise to modern researchers since pirates were not known for documenting their daily activities and since there was no advantage for said sailors to be forthcoming with honest testimony once they had been apprehended. Therefore, modern scholars have searched for historical testimony from one or more of the victims, who, needless to say, weren't available to testify—"Dead men tell no tales." But why would pirates go to the trouble to act out this charade? Why not simply give the order "Toss him overboard!"?

Again, because of the absence of insight into this folklore, we can only guess. Perhaps some captains and their crews had a superstitious notion that by forcing a person to propel himself or herself down the plank, some cosmic judge would not technically hold the pirates responsible. More likely, the pirates played out the drama for the benefit of all in attendance to serve as a warning to anyone who would dare challenge the authority of the captain. Perhaps pirates also gave some thought to enhancing their cruel reputation.

Scant evidence does exist. Francis Grose's *1811 Dictionary of the Vulgar Tongue* includes this entry: "Walking the Plank. A mode of destroying devoted persons or officers in a mutiny or ship-board, by blindfolding them, and obliging them to walk on a plank laid over the ship's side; by this means, as the mutineers suppose, avoiding the penalty of murder" (1971). Another source, though perhaps not reliable, indicates that evidence also appears in some 1789 committee minutes from a slave-trade hearing in Great Britain's House of Commons. The minutes provide the following testimony: "The food, notwithstanding the mortality, was so little, that if ten more days at sea, they should, as the captain and others said, have made the slaves walk the plank, that is, throw themselves overboard" (Great Britain, Parliament, Commons 2009).

Big Splash #1: Dismissing a Faculty Member

Fast-forward to the twenty-first century and join a group of three adults moving quickly down the hall of a school. The three come to a halt at a classroom where one enters, the teacher, followed by a man in a security guard uniform. The last member of the group, an administrator, remains outside while the guard oversees the teacher, who is haphazardly shoving her belongings into cardboard boxes.

It grieves me to acknowledge that I have heard of this scenario occurring far too often, and in some cases such drama was entirely unnecessary. Would you agree that this punitive action is a modern-day walking the plank, designed to intimidate the rest of the faculty? Why make such a big splash during the unhappy event of dismissing a faculty member? As we will see in this chapter, such behavior often leads to negative press coverage and even litigation. Can we all agree that such publicity dishonors the name of our Lord and hurts the reputation of kingdom education?

Examine the following publicized stories from four states around the country and consider what, if anything, you believe the leaders could have done differently. Could proper communication and warnings have limited the mess surrounding these dismissals and maybe even prevented the need for punitive action?

"Pregnant Teacher Sues for Unfair Dismissal"
by Georgina Fuller, *PersonnelToday.com*, November 23, 2005

At a New York City Catholic school, an unmarried teacher said she was pregnant in a conversation with the head teacher. The school dismissed the pregnant teacher. In late 2005 she planned to bring suit against the diocese of the Brooklyn school. The teacher stated publicly, "I don't understand how a religion that prides itself on forgiving and on valuing life could terminate me because I'm pregnant and choosing to have this baby."

Making this splash even larger, the New York Civil Liberties Union filed a complaint of unfair dismissal with the federal Equal Employment Opportunity Commission. The Catholic school's leaders told the teacher they were firing her because she had violated the guidelines in the personnel handbook, which states that each of its teachers must "convey the teachings of the Catholic faith by his or her words and actions."

"Court Upholds Catholic School's Right to Fire Pro-Abortion Teacher"
by John Jalsevac, *LifeSiteNews.com*, June 8, 2006

In a similar story less than a year later, a Catholic school in Wilmington, Delaware, dismissed an instructor for expressing her pro-abortion views. In this case the wake of the splash rolled all the way to the U.S. Court of Appeals for the Third Circuit after the teacher in question brought suit against Ursuline Academy of Wilmington, some of its former employees, the Catholic Diocese of Wilmington, and Bishop Michael Saltarelli. She claimed that her dismissal was sex discrimination under Title VII of the Civil Rights Act of 1964. The academy argued that she publicly denied one of the core moral values that the school exists to teach. The court ruled in favor of the defendants.

"Las Vegas Catholic School Fires Gay Teacher over MySpace Page"
by Emily Richmond, *Las Vegas Sun*, May 24, 2006

That same year a private school in Las Vegas dismissed a teacher for posting information on MySpace about his taste in movies, music, and men. The administration perceived the teacher of philosophy and film studies as agreeing with a homosexual lifestyle on the basis of his statements on MySpace.

"California Catholic School Teacher Fired After Pro-Abortion Volunteering"
by Steven Ertelt, *LifeNews.com*, October 18, 2005

A teacher at an all-girls school caused an embarrassing splash for her employers after being photographed escorting potential patients into a Planned Parenthood medical clinic. The school responded that "public participation in the procurement of abortions is morally inappropriate and unacceptable." The superintendent of the school added that teachers can hold private beliefs on controversial issues but that their public behavior cannot diametrically oppose the Catholic Church's teachings.

Three Splash Reducers in Teacher Employment: Suggestions from ACSI's *Personnel Resources for Christian Schools*

These articles certainly suggest that a big splash occurred following the dismissal of these teachers from their private schools! Probably no one reading this chapter would question the biblical principles behind the actions these schools took, but here's a fair question to ask: Did the school leaders do everything possible to prevent the negative publicity the disgruntled teachers generated? That question does not suggest that the decision itself was unavoidable, but could these school leaders have more clearly fostered their communities' understanding of and commitment to the schools' underlying core values that are based on Scripture? The following discussion emphasizes three essential ways your school can reduce the splashes from faculty dismissals.

LIFESTYLE STATEMENT

First, your school needs to adopt a lifestyle statement that articulates the expectations of the school concerning the faculty members' behavior in the school during the school day, on campus during extracurricular activities, and off campus during their personal time. Special thanks go to ACSI for including the following "Sample Lifestyle Statement" in its *Personnel Resources for Christian Schools* CD. Please note the inclusion of specific Scripture passages that serve as the foundation and source of the statement:

> *This is a sample lifestyle statement similar to what ACSI uses with its own employees. It may give your school board ideas on how to create your school's own lifestyle statement.*

_____School is a religious, nonprofit organization representing Jesus Christ throughout the local community. _____School requires its employees to be born-again Christians, living their lives as Christian role models (Romans 10:9–10, 1 Timothy 4:12, Luke 6:40). Employees will conduct themselves in a way that will not raise questions regarding their Christian testimonies. A Christian lifestyle should reflect the biblical perspective of integrity, appropriate personal and family relationships, business conduct, and moral behavior. An employee is expected to demonstrate a teachable spirit, an ability to share love for others, a willingness to live contentedly under authority, and a commitment to follow the Matthew 18 principle when an issue arises with fellow employees or management.

The _____School Statement of
Faith expects employees to maintain a lifestyle based on biblical standards of
moral conduct. Moral misconduct, which violates the bona fide occupational
qualification for employees to be Christian role models, includes, but is not
limited to, promiscuity and homosexual behavior or any other violation of the
unique roles of male and female (Romans 1:21–27, 1 Corinthians 6:9–20).
_____School believes that bibli-
cal marriage is limited to a covenant relationship between a man and a woman.

_____School employees will
maintain a lifestyle based on biblical standards of conduct. Failure to do so
may result in a reprimand or, in some cases, dismissal from employment. It
is the goal of _____School that
each employee will have a lifestyle in which "He may have the preeminence"
(Colossians 1:18, NKJV). (Carney 2009, Word document 2.2.1)

CONCEPT OF CHRISTIAN ROLE MODEL

Second, your school can reduce the negative impact that a faculty dismissal
could have by making sure the faculty members understand that each of them
is considered a Christian role model. In today's litigious climate, Christian
ministries should emphasize the phrase *Christian role model* in all their
employment materials. Schools can use contractual wording from ACSI's
Personnel Resources for Christian Schools CD. The contract language below from
ACSI communicates to a faculty member that his or her role as an instructor
goes beyond the mere presentation of information in a particular discipline or
subject area. Instead, the role includes that which the students "catch" during the
process of interacting with the teacher. Once again, please note the scriptural
basis:

> [*Print this Declaration of Moral Integrity Form on school letterhead. Attach the form
> to your applications for employment.*]

Our school expects all of its employees, as well as its volunteers who have
unsupervised access to children, to model the same Christian values and lifestyle
that it seeks to inculcate in its students. As an applicant for a ministry position
as an employee or as a volunteer at this school, I, (print name) _____
_____, recognize, understand, and agree to live
by the Christian moral standards of the school.

I declare that as a follower of Christ, I am not engaging in and commit to not engage in inappropriate sexual conduct. Inappropriate conduct includes, but is not limited to, such behaviors as the following: heterosexual activity outside of marriage (e.g., premarital sex, cohabitation, extramarital sex), homosexual activity, sexual harassment, use of (including the viewing of) pornographic material or websites, and sexual abuse or improprieties toward minors as defined by Scripture and federal or state law.

I declare that the above statement is factual and true. My signature below indicates that I meet the moral integrity standards and Christian role model lifestyle requirements of this Christian school.

_____

Applicant's signature   Date

_____

Administrator's signature *after* discussion with applicant/volunteer   Date

"Honor marriage, and guard the sacredness of sexual intimacy between wife and husband. God draws a firm line against casual and illicit sex." (Hebrews 13:4, *The Message*)

"A pupil is not superior to his teacher, but everyone [when he is] completely trained (readjusted, restored, set to rights, and perfected) will be like his teacher." (Luke 6:40, AMP) (Carney 2009, Word document 2.2.2)

Read the following description of another tragic splash that made national news and consider the concepts of lifestyle and Christian role model as each applies. Which Scripture fits most closely in each case?

"Teacher Fired, Arrested After Student Alleges Sexual Relationship"
nbcdfw.com, July 31, 2007 (article no longer available)

A private-religious-school teacher in Dallas, Texas, was arrested after a student filed a police report alleging the male teacher had a sexual relationship with her. Texas law considers the seventeen-year-old student old enough to consent to such a relationship; however, state law deems any such relationship between a student and a faculty member a second-degree felony.

School officials investigated the allegations, dismissed the faculty member, and sent letters asking for information from parents and students. The school's president stated, "The core of our mission is the care and concern of our students and that's why this is really heartbreaking for us." She also said, "I don't think there's anything more devastating than this."

MINISTRY OF TEACHING STATEMENT

Third, your school can inform its community and protect itself by ensuring that the faculty members understand they are carrying out a ministry as they each fulfill their role as a teacher overseeing the learning process. They are thus responsible for the spiritual dimension of the teaching-learning process. ACSI recommends that schools consider printing the following ministry of teaching statement (also found on the previously mentioned CD) or a similar statement in their employee handbooks and using such a statement in their staff in-service meetings:

> Teachers and school administrators are called by God to help raise up the young in the ways of faith. Jesus, the Savior, was also a teacher. He gathered His disciples and others around Him and taught with such conviction and truth that the "many who heard him were amazed. 'Where did this man get these things?' they asked. 'What's this wisdom that has been given him, that he even does miracles!'" (Mark 6:2). His apostles, likewise, were teachers, and they gave witness "with great power," through their words and their deeds, and "continued to testify to the resurrection of the Lord Jesus, and much grace was upon them all" (Acts 4:33).
>
> The ministry of teaching obligates teachers to assist their students in understanding not only the subject matter, such as mathematics or physics, but how the order and discipline of that subject matter reveal the mind of God. It obligates teachers not only to instruct in geography and history, but also to inculcate the faith by helping their students know that God created the mountains, the sea, the rivers, the deserts, the forests, the plains, and all the creatures that inhabit them, and to learn that human discoveries, empires, conflicts, and social movements are measured by the divinely ordained order. The ministry of teaching requires teachers to help their students not only to acquire skill in spelling, reading, grammar, and writing, but to understand that human language is a primary means by which students might explore the wonders of poetry and narrative and sacred Scripture itself—all of which indirectly or directly disclose salvation history. Regardless of the subject, true

teachers minister to their students by helping them follow Paul's admonition:
Finally, brothers, whatever is true, whatever is noble, whatever is right, whatever is pure, whatever is lovely, whatever is admirable— if anything is excellent or praiseworthy—think about such things. Whatever you have learned or received or heard from me, or seen in me—put it into practice. And the God of peace will be with you. (Philippians 4:8–9)

Teachers in a Christian school must be ever mindful that they instruct not only through rational explanation of formal subject material but even more powerfully through word, deed, example, and shared experience. Simply put, they teach the faith by modeling the faith and by modeling faithfulness. This is why all teachers, even before their first meeting with students, must subscribe to the school's statement of faith. This is why teachers are required to give a godly example, both at school and away. Teachers must teach truth and avoid falsehood. "Therefore each of you must put off falsehood and speak truthfully to his neighbor, for we are all members of one body.... Do not let any unwholesome talk come out of your mouths, but only what is helpful for building others up according to their needs, that it may benefit those who listen" (Ephesians 4:25–29).

Teachers minister to their students by providing them with faith experiences. They lead the youth in prayer, praise, and mercy. Paul urged Christians to "get rid of all bitterness, rage and anger, brawling and slander, along with every form of malice. Be kind and compassionate to one another, forgiving each other, just as in Christ God forgave you" (Ephesians 4:31–32). Teachers also model the Christian life by being active in their own church community and by serving as an intermediary that assists their students in becoming active in their respective church communities so that those students might be further nurtured in faith with their friends and family around them. (Carney 2009, 14–15)

Before the application of these three splash reducers to two more articles, please note this important information and advice, which can further protect your school when dismissing a faculty member:
Congress amended Title VII in 1978 by enacting the Pregnancy Discrimination Act, which expressly prohibits employers from discriminating against women on the basis of pregnancy. Firing a person for being "pregnant" is illegal. Firing a person for being "sexually active outside of marriage" is legal if it is based on the religious employment requirements of a religious employer and the employer has clearly established the prohibition as a "religious issue" in its employment

materials. Bottom line: Do not use the word *pregnant* in oral conversations or in a dismissal letter in pregnant-out-of-wedlock situations. Be sure that all of your supervisory personnel are aware of the correct way to communicate with pregnant-out-of-wedlock employees! (Carney 2009, 18)

Now please review the three main ways of reducing the splash of faculty dismissals and apply them to these two articles:

"Teacher Fired After Refusing to Allow Seventh Grader to Opt Out of Sex Ed Class"
by Hilary White, *LifeSiteNews.com*, August 11, 2006

A private school in Colorado dismissed a teacher after he ignored a parent's request to have her thirteen-year-old daughter excused from an explicit discussion about sex in her physical education class. The teacher refused to excuse the student and held a discussion on sexual practices, and he included his personal views on dating. Liberty Counsel, a pro-family, nonprofit legal organization based in Orlando, Florida, intervened on the family's behalf. Liberty Counsel's founder, Mat Staver, said, "I think teachers ought to learn a lesson from this, and that is that they are not de facto parents."

"Teacher Fired for Flashing Student"
by Kerri Webb, *Santa Barbara News Press*, May 5, 2001

A Catholic high school in California dismissed a long-term substitute teacher after she lifted up her blouse in response to a student's disparaging remarks about her teaching and the course content. In defense of her flashing her sports bra, the forty-three-year-old instructor explained, "A kid walks up to me and told me that my class is boring, so I just flashed him…. I really didn't think that I did anything wrong. There wasn't anything sexual about it. It was like me saying, 'How dare you say my class is boring.'"

The students reported the incident to other teachers who notified the administration. In her own defense the teacher argued that she considers the jogging bra more like an undershirt. Later she completely removed her shirt and waved it in protest as she exited the school parking lot.

How Can a School Leader Best Communicate the Concepts of Lifestyle, Christian Role Model, and Teaching as Ministry? To reduce the splash size of a faculty dismissal, a school leader should do everything possible to communicate that the concepts of *lifestyle*, *Christian role model*, and *teaching as ministry* reflect deeply held beliefs of the school's learning community. During appropriate occasions such as parent informational meetings, leaders should emphasize these statements publicly. Leaders should orally express these ideas during other opportunities such as teacher recruitment and interviews, faculty orientation, staff development, and teacher devotions. Written expression of these core values begins with the board, which develops institutional documents and creates policies. At the faculty level, these statements should be carefully woven into teacher contracts and handbooks, and the school should require teachers to sign a statement acknowledging that they have reviewed the core values and that they agree to abide by those values.

HELMSMAN'S LOG

Not all violations or evidence of poor performance must necessarily lead to dismissal. Leaders can certainly use other ways to communicate that changes must take place and that the school will not tolerate repetition of the behavior in question. However, as a former principal, I strongly believe that such disciplinary action must not be so severe or so damaging to the teacher's reputation with his or her peers that future growth and acceptance will be nearly impossible. Such severity was often the case in the Royal Navy when a captain ordered that a sailor undergo discipline by a procedure called keelhauling.

The sailor was tied to a rope looped beneath the vessel. Then the sailor was thrown overboard on one side of the ship and dragged under the ship's keel to the other side. Because barnacles and other marine growth often covered the hull, this punishment could result in lacerations and other injuries. Or the sailor's weight could lower him sufficiently to miss the barnacles but to drown instead. If the rope snapped, the captain might conclude that his crew did not carry out the punishment properly and might order that they repeat it. ⚓

For the larger community, the school should place effectively worded statements of these expectations on the school's website and in the school's publications.

Big Splash #2: Disciplining a Student

This chapter's second area of critical concern is the discipline, including the inevitable expulsion, of students. In some cases a long period of correction and documentation ultimately leads to the painful decision to remove a student from your school. Other times an extreme event necessitates immediate dismissal. In either case the splash and the resulting ripple effect can be enormous, particularly if the student has a long history with the school. Examine the following issues related to the discipline and even the resulting dismissal of students and consider remedies for reducing the inevitable disruption that occurs when a school takes significant disciplinary action.

Graduation Issues Causing a Splash

In a case illustrative of the turmoil surrounding student dismissals at a time close to graduation, a school in Georgia expelled a student who had attended the school for thirteen years and who was supposed to graduate in just days. The student had violated the school's honor code by cheating and earlier in her senior year by the "intent to cheat." In late April the senior was taking a make-up test when two faculty members caught her discussing with another student how to do one of the math problems. Upon receiving notice of the expulsion, her parents filed suit, claiming a breach of contract and a breach of fundamental fairness and due process (Carney 2007, 16). The case went all the way to the Court of Appeals of Georgia. The justices sided with the school and supported the administration's right to dismiss a student in that situation, regardless of the student's upcoming graduation. The judges concluded, "The action of expulsion, under the facts and circumstances of this case, was not arbitrary or capricious, but a reasonable exercise of administrative and academic discretion, based upon the reasonable belief at the time of the second offense and the silence of [the student by not appealing the first offense] that she had committed two honor code violations; where the exercise of discretion is to be judged, it is judged not by hindsight but the knowledge of the moment of decision. There was no violation of fundamental fairness in the treatment of [the student]" (Carney 2007, 21).

In some disciplinary situations, difficult confrontations appear inevitable, even after a school gives prior warnings. Such was the case in a much-publicized graduation event in which public-school officials withheld the diplomas of several graduates.

The Associated Press article "Diplomas Denied over Graduation Cheers" (*New York Times*, June 3, 2007) reports that five students crossed the stage of their graduation ceremony in Illinois and returned to their seats empty-handed. The school denied the students their diplomas because their families and friends in attendance defied a ban on loud celebrations. School officials, because of past disruptions during a graduation ceremony, had asked students and their parents the week before graduation to sign a contract promising to act in a dignified way.

"It was like one of the worst days of my life," said Caisha Gayles, one of the five students. "You walk across the stage and then you can't get your diploma because of other people cheering for you. It was devastating." To receive their diplomas, the five students had to complete eight hours of public service such as answering phones and sorting books for the district.

I encourage you as an administrator to consider what you and other community leaders could have done to reduce the conflict and the resulting ill will that stained this ceremony. The exhortation of the chapter is not to shrink back from justifiable execution of your disciplinary procedures but to give serious consideration to lowering the temperature of heated conflict and reducing the negative repercussions.

No time in the educational life of students produces the heightened stress and high expectations of the final semester leading up to senior-high-school graduation. It is not surprising, therefore, that few disciplinary decisions garner as much attention and create as many disruptive waves as those that involve the perceived right to graduate from the school a student is attending, regardless of the student's infraction.

Two recent examples captured national attention. The article "3 Seniors Expelled over Sex Tape" (*News4Jax.com*, April 17, 2009) reports that a Christian school expelled three students in Jacksonville, Florida, for making a movie that administrators determined inappropriate for a member of their student body. A spokesperson for the school explained, "Clearly it violates the values, which are the foundation and the structure of our academy." The disciplinary decision, made less than two months before graduation, was in line with the school's student handbook, which states that "[an act] of immorality on or off campus ... results in expulsion." The spokesperson added that the school was taking steps to help the students both spiritually and academically. Another publicized case appeared in the RNS Newsroom Solutions article "HS Student Suspended for Attending Other School's Prom" (*ArkansasMatters.com*, May 12, 2009). An Ohio Christian school suspended a senior because he accompanied his girlfriend to her prom at a local public school, in opposition to the Christian school's rules and to a warning from its administration. The school's student handbook prohibits dancing, rock music, and hand-holding. The school still allowed the senior to take his exams and receive his diploma, although he could not participate in the graduation ceremony. The big splash surrounding the school's decision included the consideration of a lawsuit by the student's father and an invitation to the young man to appear on *Inside Edition* and ABC's *Primetime*.

As I have stated throughout this discussion, no one involved in Christian schooling would argue whether these private schools have the right to enforce—during the time up to and including graduation day—the policies and rules that appear in their school documents. The decision making in these two publicized cases seems to suggest that the administrators were trying to soften the blow of dismissal because the violators were seniors. In both cases, the schools made provisions to allow the students to complete the requirements necessary for them to receive their high-school diplomas. It appears prudent to this experienced administrator that the leaders were faithful to their policies while at the same time balancing what was best for the individuals involved. In the larger picture the Christian school movement does not need a constant barrage of legal suits taken to judges who, in the past, have expressed strong interest in staying out of the day-to-day decision making of school officials. If we take advantage of this judicial tradition, however, and act in ways that appear mean-spirited or capricious, then this reluctance to be involved will erode.

Technology Issues Causing a Splash

The first decade of the twenty-first century produced unprecedented advances in technological communication, and with these came the need for new school policies that ensure a school's security and safety while allowing the convenience and even the educational value of these new inventions. It is fascinating to research the variety of approaches that schools, both Christian and public, take to dealing with these challenges and with the resulting need to discipline students. Let's explore some of the major issues.

By the time of this chapter's publication, it is safe to say that every school has a written policy concerning students' possession and use of cell phones. As an experienced teacher and administrator, I want to encourage you to rethink the prohibition of cell phone use during the school day. What is the overall goal of your procedures and discipline? I believe that the goal is to teach self-discipline so that students become independent, self-managed learners. I have chosen to omit the name and place of a school that takes the time and undergoes the administrative hassle to collect every student's cell phone each morning in a separate plastic lunch bag where it remains in the office during the day. The school officials initiated this procedure after two occurrences of students' sending text messages with test answers during an exam. Such a reaction sends the unwritten message that a small number of dishonest students can override the honorable, trustworthy behavior of the many. Second, the reaction says that students are not capable of influencing their classmates—through positive peer pressure—to strive for excellence in integrity. Third, the educators are missing the opportunity to train students in the appropriate use of new technologies, skills that a rapidly changing society will demand of the students. I recommend a more-balanced approach that requires students to keep their cell phones in their lockers and gives the students the option to use them with permission of a faculty member during the school day.

The banning of cell phones in public schools has received a great deal of attention in the media. In the article "Parents Lose in Court Case on Cell Phones" (*New York Sun*, May 8, 2007), Sarah Garland writes about a group of parents in New York City who challenged Mayor Bloomberg's ban on cell phones in city schools. The case went all the way to the state supreme court, where a judge decided to dismiss the case. Garland notes that "in the lawsuit, the plaintiffs had argued that the ban on the possession of cell phones violates the constitutional rights of students, although they had conceded that a ban on the use of phones in schools was justified."

The addition of camera technology to students' cell phones has added a new layer of difficulty and complexity to this discussion on technology and the related discipline of students. Not surprising to anyone, student use of camera phones has included taking pictures of tests, school documents, school records, and classmates in locker rooms and bathrooms without their permission. Such disruptions and privacy violations have led the Christian Law Association in Seminole, Florida, to recommend the following policy:

General Policy: Students are not permitted to use a cell phone in the school building before or during school time. After school, students should not use cell phones until they have left the school building.

Any use of a cell phone in school during school hours by a student will result in disciplinary action. If a student brings a cell phone to school, the cell phone must be secured in the student's locker and must be turned off. If a student brings a cell phone to class or the phone rings while in a student's locker, the teacher will initiate disciplinary action and the phone may be confiscated for the remainder of the day. (Confiscated phones may be returned by the administration to parents upon request. Students whose phones have been confiscated may be asked not to bring a cell phone to school in the future.)

Note: "Forgetting" to turn off the cell phone is not an excuse.

Use of a cell phone during a test for any reason ... will automatically be considered cheating, and appropriate academic and disciplinary action will be taken in the sole discretion of the administration.

No taking of or other use of cell phone photographs/videos is permitted during the school day. Particularly, no cell phone photographs/videos are permitted in the restrooms or locker room areas at any time. Violation of this prohibition is a serious discipline offense.

Because modern cell phones may also function as data storage devices, student cell phones brought to school are subject to inspection and review by school staff pursuant to the ministry's normal search & seizure policy and administrative discretion. Any contraband content or content deemed to be inappropriate in the sole discretion of the administration may be grounds for further discipline.

Parents who need to contact their child during the school day for emergency purposes should use the school's normal emergency contact process and call the main school phone number. School staff will assist parents in communicating with their child in appropriate emergency situations. Parents should not consider their child's cell phone as a means of contacting their child for any reason during the school day.

Note: These guidelines were formulated after careful review of school cell phone policies across the State and the country. (2006)

I want to call your attention to the portion of this policy recommendation that mentions the inspection of a student's phone, including the information and communications stored on the phone. Recent legal discussions necessitate that school officials specifically consider whether they intend to examine the contents of students' cell phones. This sensitive and already complex portion of school law known as search-and-seizure procedures became even more difficult and contentious when school administrators in Colorado transcribed text messages from students' confiscated cell phones. In the article "Phone Searches Spark Protest" (*Rocky Mountain News*, October 11, 2007), Sue Lindsay writes about one instance at the heart of the discussion. A security officer accused a student of smoking. According to the account by the ACLU, in the principal's office an administrator asked the student to empty his pockets but found no cigarettes. The administrator then took the student's cell phone and left the office, only to return and report that he had found incriminating text messages that mentioned marijuana. The ACLU of Colorado maintained that if a student is accused of smoking, for example, administrators have a right to see what's in the student's pockets or backpack, but in this case, "once they found nothing in the pockets or backpack, the administrators should have stopped."

Another serious issue related to technology is cyberbullying, a concern that is on the rise because of the availability of technology to nearly every school-age child. Ted Feinberg and Nicole Robey, both of whom work in the field of school psychology, define the term this way: "Cyberbullying involves sending or posting harmful or cruel text or images using the Internet (e.g., instant messaging, e-mails, chat rooms, and social networking sites) or other digital communication devices, such as cell phones. It can involve stalking, threats, harassment, impersonation, humiliation, trickery, and exclusion" (2008, 10).

These researchers point out that the destructive consequences for victims of cyberbullying can be equal to or even more damaging than face-to-face bullying. Feinberg and Robey urge schools to incorporate cyberbullying into all their relevant school policies; educate students, parents, and staff members about the issue; instruct students how to be Internet savvy; investigate every report of cyberbullying; support the students who are victims or perpetrators; and understand the relevant legal obligations and restrictions (2008, 12–13). Christian educator Jeffrey Sheppard concludes his article on this topic with an appropriate challenge to protect and to discipline: "It is important that we as Christian educators and administrators pursue both the protection of those who may be hurt and the consequences for those who inflict harm—with a foundation of love, for love truly does cover a multitude of sins" (2006–2007, 45).

The emergence of "sexting"—sending or receiving nude or semi-nude digital photographs—has added to the maelstrom of controversy over student discipline related to technology. In the article "Should 'Sexting' Teens Be Charged as Sex Offenders and Felons?" (*Christianity.com*), Jim Liebelt explains that "in some cases, the photos are sent to harass other teens or to get attention. Other times, they're viewed as a high-tech way to flirt." But just the article's title itself suggests the seriousness with which some public officials are taking this activity. A January 2009 case in Pennsylvania received publicity in Mike Brunker's article " 'Sexting' Surprise: Teens Face Child Porn Charges" (*msnbc.com*, January 15, 2009). Police charged three female students with manufacturing, disseminating, or possessing child pornography after they took nude or semi-nude photos of themselves and passed them to male classmates by using cell phones. The boys face charges of possession. The police captain explained, "It's very dangerous.... Once it's on a cell phone, that cell phone can be put on the Internet where everyone in the world can get access to that juvenile picture. You don't realize what you are doing until it's already done." With this exhortation in mind, Christian school administrators must be diligent in using technology instruction to teach their students about these dangers. It is disheartening both to imagine the publicity surrounding an incident like this in a Christian school and to think of the wounds to a student, the family, the learning community, and, most important, the cause of Christ.

And a final warning about the big splash of student discipline related to technology arises from the decisions about punishing a student for questionable material on that student's home website. Burt Carney, former ACSI director for legal/legislative issues, wrote the article "Can a Student Be Expelled for Having an Inappropriate Home Website?" Carney reviews a New York case in which the parents of a Catholic-high-school student sued their son's former school after it dismissed him for placing what the school considered "questionable material" on his personal website and inviting other students to visit the site. The parents argued that the school "violated their son's free speech, due process, and possibly privacy rights, and they sued the school for $1 million" (2006, 18). The district court judge in the case ruled that for the plaintiffs to argue a violation of First or Fourteenth Amendment rights, they must establish that the violation resulted from state action. The court said that private-school administrators do not carry out "acts of the state." Carney goes on to explain that a school does have the right to dismiss because of a student's home website but should do so only after consultation with its attorney (22). Carney includes this overall advice:

> It's also wise to have a robust school student code of conduct or student lifestyle statement (student code) that clearly indicates your school's endeavor to develop the whole student with an integrated Christian lifestyle. The student code should indicate that your school seeks to avoid the commonplace situation in which students act one way at church or school, but another way on their own time. Clearly state that it is your school's expectation that a student honor Christ in all behavior and activities 24/7/365. Be sure to put the 365 in so that vacation periods will also be covered between school years! (23)

The Christian Law Association recommends the following wording for a policy regarding students' personal websites:

> Any student who decides to operate a personal online website or contributes to a blog must register the website/blog with the pastoral staff.... The website must be registered immediately upon its creation. Any student who creates a website or blog prior to attending the Academy must register the website/blog as soon as he/she is accepted as a student. All websites/blogs will be monitored for content on a regular basis. Any student, including home school students, found with an

unregistered website/blog or website/blog material that is deemed inappropriate to the purpose and mission of the Academy will be in direct disobedience to this ruling and will be subject to disciplinary action up to and including immediate ineligibility to attend the Academy. (Gibbs Law Firm 2010, 11)

Serious discussions about moral obligations, security, privacy, and legalities need to take place before a school creates student and faculty policy manuals. After receiving current legal advice from a local attorney familiar with these issues, a school's administration should advise the community of the policies in as many forums and through as many media as possible.

The following incident shows the significant negative publicity and the distraction of legal action that can result from a leader's decision to dismiss high-school students because of inappropriate and unbiblical sexual behavior. The article "Lesbian Suit Against Christian School Tossed" (*WorldNetDaily.com*, January 25, 2008) reports that early in 2008 a California judge ruled that a Christian school did not discriminate against two female students when the administrator dismissed them for engaging in homosexual behavior. In reaction to the dismissal, in 2005 the families brought a suit that alleged discrimination, invasion of privacy, and unfair business practices in the school's handling and ultimate dismissal of the girls, who were juniors at the time. The lawsuit claimed that the principal interrogated the girls in separate rooms without their parents and that he asked inappropriate questions of a personal nature. The following day, the administrator called the parents to inform them of the board's decision to dismiss the girls, and he wrote a letter to the parents explaining that there appeared to be a bond of intimacy that suggested a lesbian relationship even absent evidence of physical contact between the girls. The school leadership determined that such appearances were not in agreement with the school's values and beliefs.

Representatives of the Christian Legal Society and of the Alliance Defense Fund argued on behalf of the school. The arguments in favor of the school stated, "The 14th Amendment protects the right of parents to send their children to a private religious school that shares their religious beliefs…. The United States Supreme Court has long recognized the existence of parents' right to direct their children's education." The court filings on behalf of the school also explained that the state may use licensing and reporting requirements to govern the "basic requirements" of private schools but that "it cannot unreasonably interfere with the teaching and educational philosophies of such schools."

How would your school handle a similar case? Just how major would the splash become? Have your student handbooks, parent communications, discipline procedures, and current practices prepared you to defend such a legal challenge to a student dismissal?

Big Splash #3: You—Being Dismissed Yourself

During the writing of this chapter it occurred to me that many veteran leaders would respond, "When you wrote 'Walking the Plank,' I thought you were referring to the administrator!" I have a number of friends who each have a heartbreaking story about being blindsided by a single authority figure or a board that communicated the administrator's sudden dismissal without prior warning, a chance to grow and improve, or even the opportunity for rebuttal. How can a school's leadership avoid this tidal wave of disruption in the life of the school?

Primarily, the most significant step needs to take place early on, one in which the administrator and his or her board agree upon a professional, orderly, and God-honoring procedure for an annual evaluation. That document must include clear steps for carrying out the process, a list of objectives to be achieved that are connected to the job description, and clear indications of data sources for assessing the administrator's performance. Second, by including an arbitration agreement like the one in the appendix, a school can constructively limit the big splash of sudden dismissal. It is worth noting that the document in the appendix would be a good starting point for considering an arbitration agreement for all employees. In advance of disagreement or disharmony, both parties agree to a prescribed process, and they agree to submit to that process. This arbitration agreement includes the use of a third-party arbiter and the stated intention to abide by his or her decision rather than begin proceedings in a court of law.

Consider this collision that occurred in my friend's life in early 2010. After a successful tenure for three years, my administrator friend was informed on a Friday in late winter that he was dismissed from his employment at the school, having received no prior warning or notice. The following day a letter arrived at the home of each student, explaining the coming changes. After thanking the outgoing administrator for his leadership, which was instrumental in the school's rapid growth, the author of the letter went on to state mysteriously that the board thought it best to "go in a different direction" and that it would begin a search for a new school leader. The board would divide the duties of the head of school into small chunks and assign them to various staff members until the board hired a new head of school. Do I need to tell you that the unsuspecting parents did not receive these changes well? But how should this administrator have responded, and how should others like him respond? Firestorm? Legal action? Start a new school immediately?

I believe that an outgoing leader, whether leaving for failures on his or her part or for reasons entirely unfair, has significant responsibility to depart with dignity and with respect for the Lord, the children, the community that supports the school, and the office of head of school itself. Consider Paul's exhortation in Romans 12:18: "If possible, so far as it depends on you, be at peace with all men." And Paul, no stranger to conflict and chaos, urges us very appropriately in a paragraph from *The Message*: "Since God has so generously let us in on what he is doing, we're not about to throw up our hands and walk off the job just because we run into occasional hard times. We refuse to wear masks and play games. We don't maneuver and manipulate behind the scenes. And we don't twist God's Word to suit ourselves. Rather, we keep everything we do and say out in the open, the whole truth on display, so that those who want to can see and judge for themselves in the presence of God" (2 Corinthians 4:1–2).

Are you facing such a situation in your ministry now, or do you have some old wounds or battle scars from that kind of dismissal? I conclude this chapter with the words of Paul, who knew full well the cost of discipleship. I encourage you to let these words sink deep into your heart and to allow God's immeasurable love to wash over you: "So, as those who have been chosen of God, holy and beloved, put on a heart of compassion, kindness, humility, gentleness and patience; bearing with one another, and forgiving each other, whoever has a complaint against anyone; just as the Lord forgave you, so also should you. Beyond all these things put on love, which is the perfect bond of unity. Let the peace of Christ rule [literally *act as arbiter*] in your hearts, to which indeed you were called in one body; and be thankful" (Colossians 3:12–15).

HELMSMAN'S LOG

Read the following article about a teacher's dismissal from a Christian school and consider these events in light of this chapter's suggestions. Could you have made the splash any smaller?

"Teacher Says She Was Fired Because of Hairstyle"
WSBTV.com, October 26, 2006

In the Atlanta area the leaders of a Christian school dismissed a female teacher because they told her, according to the teacher, that her "hairstyle does not fit the image of the school."

The third-grade teacher said that before the day of her firing she had received no negative comments related to her job performance. Another aspect of the dismissal that the teacher noted as upsetting was that her hairstyle on the day the school hired her was similar to the one she had the day the school fired her, just shorter in length.

After this experience the teacher initially wanted only an apology, but later she considered filing a lawsuit. ⚓

Fighting Broadsides
Administrator and Board, Confronting in Love

The most formidable problem facing Christian schools today

◆ Biblical rules of engagement for the administrator: 1 Thessalonians 5:12–22

◆ Biblical rules of engagement for the school board: 1 Peter 5:1–10

◆ Survival techniques for fighting broadsides

All students of American history recall studying the brave words of John Paul Jones, but most, however, are not aware of the circumstances surrounding this battle cry: "I have not yet begun to fight!" Jones was the captain of the Continental Navy ship *Bonhomme Richard* when he engaged British Navy ships off the coast of England near Flamborough Head on September 23, 1779. Jones had renamed this converted warship in honor of Benjamin Franklin, whose book *Poor Richard's Almanack* had been translated into French, having the title *Les Maximes du Bonhomme Richard*. Before the battle, Captain Richard Pearson of the HMS *Serapis*, with his own hands, nailed the British ensign, or colors, to the mast. Nailing an ensign to a mast expressed defiance and meant that a ship would never strike its colors—that is, the ship would never surrender. Jones later matched Pearson's hubris, however. Because the *Serapis* had superior fire power, Jones had to maneuver the *Bonhomme Richard* skillfully and lash her to the *Serapis*. During the battle, the British shot away the *Bonhomme Richard*'s main mast, which carried the ship's ensign. Because the flag was no longer flying, Pearson then asked Jones if Jones had struck. Jones is said to have responded, "I have not yet begun to fight!" Jones finally won the battle even though the *Bonhomme Richard*, badly damaged, later sank. After Jones returned to America in 1781, Congress passed a vote of thanks to him for the way he had preserved the honor of the American fleet and in 1787 awarded him a gold medal (NHC 2003; John Paul Jones Museum).

Could this vow of determination—I have not yet begun to fight—be heard in one of your board meetings? Are there one or more individuals in the group hoping to see the administrator strike his or her colors as a sign of submission and surrender? Or have you as the school's leader already determined that you will not yield under any circumstances, and you have, therefore, symbolically nailed your colors to the mast? The theme of this chapter is a clarion call to all those in leadership both to search the Word of God for His instructions for their "rules of engagement" and to beseech the Holy Spirit to tutor the hearts of the school's leaders in the lessons of Christlike ways to deal with conflict. Take a step back and consider your actions in any conflict in which you are embroiled. Have you lashed your ship of ideas to another's and determined that one or both vessels can sink before you surrender? We will examine two New Testament passages, the first providing a focus for the administrator and the second providing a focus for the school board.

RULES OF ENGAGEMENT FOR THE ADMINISTRATOR

The apostle Paul was no stranger to conflict and uproar. It's been said that wherever he went, a revival or a riot broke out, and often both. Such was the case for the young church at Thessalonica, where Paul was run out of town after a short but successful ministry (Acts 17:1–10). He wrote to encourage the new believers to conduct their lives in such a way that they would glorify the Lord and not themselves. Here are some of his instructions:

> Now we ask you, brothers, to respect those who work hard among you, who are over you in the Lord and who admonish you. Hold them in the highest regard in love because of their work. Live in peace with each other. And we urge you, brothers, warn those who are idle, encourage the timid, help the weak, be patient with everyone. Make sure that nobody pays back wrong for wrong, but always try to be kind to each other and to everyone else.
>
> Be joyful always; pray continually; give thanks in all circumstances, for this is God's will for you in Christ Jesus.
>
> Do not put out the Spirit's fire; do not treat prophecies with contempt. Test everything. Hold on to the good. Avoid every kind of evil. (1 Thessalonians 5:12–22, NIV)

Let's highlight a few key imperatives to remember:
+ Respect those who are over you and who admonish you.
+ Hold them in highest regard.
+ Live in peace with each other.
+ Be patient with everyone.
+ Do not repay a wrong with a wrong.
+ Be kind to each other.
+ Be joyful always.
+ Pray continually.
+ Give thanks in all circumstances.
+ Do not put out the Spirit's fire.
+ Hold on to the good.
+ Avoid every kind of evil.

A dozen imperatives for all leaders to follow! There will be numerous times you feel threatened or hemmed in or manipulated, but Paul instructs you not to give in to the "natural man" (1 Corinthians 2:14) and the tendency to retaliate. I encourage you to meditate on these commands and prayerfully consider these words and phrases: *respect, hold in highest regard, live in peace, be patient, do not repay a wrong, be kind, continually pray and give thanks, hold on to good,* and *avoid evil.* When administrators fail to conduct themselves in this manner, I am reminded of the closing words of Marc Antony following his funeral speech in *Julius Caesar.* Marc Antony spoke in the context of his confrontation with those who conspired to kill Caesar: "Cry 'Havoc!' and let slip the dogs of war!" Such a carnal approach in Christian ministry both dishonors the sufferings of Christ and wounds many innocents who become collateral damage in leadership struggles.

Rules of Engagement for the School Board

In 1 Peter, the apostle Peter addresses new Christians who are undergoing tremendous pressure and persecution in Asia Minor. He challenges them to live lives of holiness that befit the grace they have received from the Lord Jesus. Let's examine this powerful passage that specifically speaks to those who are leaders, entrusted with the welfare of others:

> To the elders among you, I appeal as a fellow elder, a witness of Christ's sufferings and one who also will share in the glory to be revealed: Be shepherds of God's flock that is under your care, serving as overseers—not because you must, but because you are willing, as God wants you to be; not greedy for money, but eager to serve; not lording it over those entrusted to you, but being examples to the flock. And when the Chief Shepherd appears, you will receive the crown of glory that will never fade away.
>
> Young men, in the same way be submissive to those who are older. All of you, clothe yourselves with humility toward one another, because,
>
> "God opposes the proud
> but gives grace to the humble."
>
> Humble yourselves, therefore, under God's mighty hand, that he may lift you up in due time. Cast all your anxiety on him because he cares for you.
>
> Be self-controlled and alert. Your enemy the devil prowls around like a roaring lion looking for someone to devour. Resist him, standing firm in the faith, because you know that your brothers throughout the world are undergoing the same kind of sufferings.
>
> And the God of all grace, who called you to his eternal glory in Christ, after you have suffered a little while, will himself restore you and make you strong, firm and steadfast. (1 Peter 5:1–10, NIV)

Once again, let's highlight some key commands:

+ Be shepherds of God's flock.
+ Serve willingly and eagerly.
+ Be examples to your followers.
+ Clothe yourselves with humility.
+ Cast all your anxiety on the Lord.
+ Be self-controlled and alert.
+ Resist Satan.
+ Stand firm in your faith.

Can you imagine the sweet fellowship and harmony that would pervade every board meeting if all the members would commit to such behavior? Review these commands that challenge you to Christian maturity: *be shepherds, serve willingly, be examples, put on humility, cast your anxiety on the Lord, be self-controlled,*

HELMSMAN'S LOG

TEN COMMANDMENTS FOR SCHOOL BOARD MEMBERS

1. "Do not administrate. Board members determine the direction of the organization and act as facilitators."
2. "Do not fail to provide adequate resources (facilities, funds, or personnel) to enable your established programs and goals."
3. "Do not fail to set clear policies for the administration to follow."
4. "Do not allow individuals who lack a strong commitment to Christian school education to serve on the board."
5. "Do not allow a board member who fails to attend regularly scheduled meetings to remain on the board."
6. "Do not set a budget based on the 'assumption' that the school's enrollment will grow by a certain percentage."
7. "Do not allow individuals to address the board until the appropriate staff members are aware of the specific issue(s) and the proper chain-of-command has been followed."

HELMSMAN'S LOG

8. "Do not allow the faculty or staff to perform annual reviews of the administration (superintendent/administrator)."
9. "Do not put off praying over difficult decisions. If good solutions are not found in a timely manner, stop the discussion at the meeting to pray specifically for the Lord's direction."
10. "Do not hold meetings dealing with the school's operation without the presence of the senior administrator unless you are discussing his/her compensation package or performance review." (Davidson 1998–1999, 10) ⚓

resist Satan, and *stand firm.* This is the standard for the high calling of leadership of a Christian ministry. Christian school leaders cannot do less!

How can board members demonstrate these biblical qualities? Here are some examples:

+ Agree not to ambush the head of school in a meeting by bringing up matters for discussion that are not listed on the agenda or by giving reports about issues that are not listed on the agenda.
+ Do not participate in another form of ambush by asking a leading question that puts the administrator in a bad light, particularly if you have information that has not already been brought to the administrator's attention regarding the topic. For instance, a principal was once asked a question by a board member who predicted that the leader would not know the answer. After a few difficult moments, the questioner pulled from his briefcase a document that contained the answer to the question he had asked.
+ Resist Satan's temptation to be jealous of the attention and prestige that the school's administrator naturally accrues. The school must have a "face," a public personality that the community relates to daily. Many shipwrecks occur because one board member, often the chair, feels as if he must wrest control of the helm from the administrator who has been called to lead the ministry to achieve its mission.

+ Refuse to "gunnysack" grievances that various people have against the school's administrator. This practice usually culminates when the board chair, with or without the knowledge and participation of the rest of the board, calls the leader into a meeting at which the chair dumps the gunnysack of bad reports on the table.
+ Refuse to be a collector or conduit of bad reports. Some board members have a hero complex or enjoy being a fix-it person, gladly receiving information about disagreements regarding the school, its faculty, or the administrator. (See letter to a concerned parent.)

HELMSMAN'S LOG

READING THE TELLTALES

Telltales are streamers usually made of nylon about six to twelve inches long. Attached to the sails, telltales give information to the helmsman and the crew about wind in the sails and the direction of the ship. The helmsman steers by a compass or to a fixed point in the horizon, and it is the crew members' duty to keep trimming the sails so that the telltales stream in the proper direction (WB-Sails 1998). The ways a board handles conflict and disagreements with the school's head can serve as telltales of its leadership strength, of the force of the Holy Spirit's wind in the direction the school is headed, and of the school's potential to make its vision a reality. ⚓

Responding Appropriately When Approached with a Problem

Dear Concerned Parent,

All of us involved at Anytown Christian School seek to glorify the Lord as we serve each family to the very best of our ability. The matter of _____ that you have brought to my attention is certainly a concern to me as it is to you.

We have searched the Scriptures for biblical directions for dealing with disagreements, and it is our practice to follow Matthew 18 in any situation in which an individual finds it necessary to question the decision, speech, or action of another. We want to encourage you to approach those involved in a loving and candid spirit. It is our expectation that all those in our school community will receive a brother or a sister in Christ with an open mind and a loving spirit.

If you have not already approached those involved, I would ask you to do so. If you have and you believe further discussion is needed, then the next step is to involve the principal who oversees your child's division in the school and enlist his or her advice.

I meet with the headmaster regularly and will call the matter to his attention in our next meeting. Each time we meet, we pray for the school and about the individual challenges we are aware of, asking for God's grace and discernment in every situation. We also take seriously the two greatest commandments, to love God and to love others as ourselves. In the meantime, if you wish to approach the teacher or the principal as I suggested above, then I think this would be a good idea.

Please continue to pray for the leadership of our school as we serve the Lord and your children.

Chair of the School Board

Notes Relating to this Letter

Paragraph one. Assure the parent that you want the best for everyone involved, but stop short of saying, "Thank you for contacting me." It is a delicate but extremely important balance. For whatever reason, the concerned parent may not have chosen to communicate with the person or persons closest to the problem. On the other hand, perhaps the parent did, and the result was not satisfactory. At this point what might appear to be a stone wall of protection or indifference is more damaging than a breach in protocol. The issue can be dealt with in the future if need be, and at this point the relationship is not irreparably damaged. On the other hand, a response that communicates "I can be your problem solver; feel free to contact me in the future" will undermine the credibility of all those in the chain of command.

Paragraphs two and three. Gently review with the concerned parent the scriptural basis of the Matthew 18 process and recommend specific steps, which the parent may or may not have attempted. Present the main concepts in a straightforward way without sounding condescending or pharisaical.

Paragraph four. Return to the balance between acknowledging a genuine problem that needs some degree of attention and the importance of knowing the authority of those charged with the responsibility in the area of concern. State that you will not act in an ultra vires manner, that is, in a manner beyond the scope of your authority. Tell the concerned parent that the headmaster will be involved in the situation and that the parent can have confidence that the problem will be dealt with in a compassionate way.

John Schimmer, one of the most experienced school leaders in the field of governance, describes the challenge that board members who are parents face as they balance their loyalties, especially if those board members serve in church-sponsored schools:

> Many Christian schools represent the ministry of a local church, further complicating the trustee's role. Trustees worship and socialize weekly with faculty, parents, and students who perceive them as having "authority." Trustees must listen well but refer all matters to the school staff....
>
> Confidentiality is absolutely essential in board deliberations. Dissent is healthy inside the meeting, but once a vote is taken, the board speaks as ONE VOICE. To put it another way, all board members speak within the board room, but only one person, usually the chair, speaks outside the meeting. When board members willingly surrender personal agendas and biases to the good of the body and submit themselves to the guidance of Scripture, the board will enjoy unity of purpose and mission. (1998–1999, 32; emphasis in original)

One of the best-known and most admired Christian school leaders of the last half of the twentieth century was Roy W. Lowrie Jr. In the book *Serving God on the Christian School Board*, he and his son, Roy L. Lowrie, echo the theme of this chapter: being biblical in your responsiveness to parents and in your support for those who lead and teach in the school every day. The Lowries emphasize the value of knowing and valuing what parents are thinking while not giving them the impression that the parent majority rules and that votes from participating families will decide policy. "A good board will never run roughshod over the parents, but over time it will make, for the good of the school, some difficult decisions that may be unpopular with some parents and perhaps most of them." The Lowries exhort board members to be circumspect in their behavior and conversation:

> Members of a board need to be discreet about listening to and talking with parents. The Bible's warning that people in authority must not talk too much applies here. Loose words spoken by a board member carry the weight of authority and have a way of becoming known to many people. A board member

who is a whisperer, a gossip, or a talebearer damages the ministry of the school deeply. If that member does not change within a reasonable time after being reproved by the board chair, he or she should be removed from the board. The problems that such a member causes cannot be tolerated. (2004, 54)

HELMSMAN'S LOG

In light of the discussion on rules of engagement, consider this case study from Kenn Gangel's book *Surviving Toxic Leaders: How to Work for Flawed People in Churches, Schools, and Christian Organizations*:

W. J. McCalkin lived a wealthy but irritated life. Determined to send his children to a Christian school, he became very upset upon discovering that none existed in his area, so he decided to build one. Not to start one, but to build one. He bought a piece of land, had a building erected with several classrooms, and opened the doors.

After about two years McCalkin noticed that the growth factor seemed to slow down even though the school did not yet have 100 students. He had named himself chairman of the board and selected other board members, so in every sense this was what educators call a "proprietary institution." Wisely, he and the other board members decided to search for a principal. They contacted a Christian graduate school nearby and hired the first candidate they interviewed. The new principal had approximately ten years' experience in the classroom and two years' internship in administration, as well as a Master's degree in Educational Administration.

Voila! A perfect marriage. The school began to grow; the parents were excited; the upper half of the building was completed and almost immediately filled—one would think McCalkin's dream had come true.

But a subtle change took place along the way. The new principal (we'll call him Sam), because of his everyday presence among the students and at all parental events, logically became the head of the school, something McCalkin had not figured into the equation.

HELMSMAN'S LOG

No one was at fault. It would be highly unusual in any school for parents and students to think of the Chairman of the Board rather than the principal as the chief leader of the school.

At the very point he felt those pangs of jealousy, McCalkin could have talked with Sam irenically and worked out some kind of satisfactory compromise. Instead, he said nothing, while deceptively planning behind the principal's back to attack him one day off campus with a portion of the board and tell him he must resign immediately. So immediately, in fact, that they locked his office door and he could not return to the building to gather his own belongings. (2008, 9) ⚓

The Lowries are also precise and insightful in their recommendation that every school have an established grievance policy that it clearly communicates to all members of the school community. Misunderstandings and differences of opinion are everyday facts of life, even among the smallest, most congenial groups. How we deal with these challenges sets us in the Christian community apart from all other communities. Unfortunately, many parents have not received proper instruction in this important dimension of Christian ethics, or they allow Satan, their natural tendencies, or both to overcome their consciences. Therefore, leaders must develop, discuss, and implement procedures such as those the Lowries suggest:

The steps for handling a parent complaint about a teacher or a teacher complaint about a parent follow the [Matthew 18] pattern:

+ The parent meets privately with the teacher to seek a resolution in a spirit of reconciliation.
+ If there is no resolution, the parent takes another neutral adult and meets with the teacher in the spirit of reconciliation.
+ If there is no resolution, the parent meets with the teacher and the administrator to seek a resolution in a spirit of reconciliation.
+ If there still is no resolution, in some schools, the problem may be presented to the entire school board, which then calls upon the parties involved as seems warranted, all in a spirit of reconciliation. (2004, 54–55)

Helmsman's Log

A Standard of Love
for All Those in the School Community

Jesus spoke often of the prime directive for us His followers: we are to love one another. The New Testament describes two specific ways we can demonstrate our commitment to this standard. First, we can do so by *confronting in love*. Both Matthew 5:22–24 and Matthew 18:15–17 mandate that believers take the initiative to reconcile with anyone who has offended them or whom they may have offended. We must not show indifference or shift blame. We who are strong need to take the responsibility for restoration. But do we go about looking to ferret out every little slight or offense that comes our way?

The apostle Peter presents the second love principle: *covering in love*. In 1 Peter 4:8 he writes, "Above all, keep fervent in your love for one another, because love covers a multitude of sins" (see also Proverbs 10:12 and 1 Corinthians 13:5). As often as we can, we are urged to cover over grievances and genuinely forgive the one who has offended. Of course our forgiveness takes maturity and discernment in that some wrongdoing only becomes worse when someone does not confront it. ⚓

From the Author's Heart:
Survival Techniques for Fighting Broadsides

Administrator, are you struggling with a board or some individual board members who are stifling your ambitions for the school? Meditate on 1 Thessalonians 5:12–22 and consider that the Lord has placed these men and women in authority over you for His purposes. It could be that they are more discerning in this situation and that they are following God's timing. Or it could be that they are just flat wrong but that the Lord is teaching you patience and humility through this test. Why must you insist on having things your way? Are you bored with the resources and activities at your disposal? Do you have a master plan in your head and they are slowing you down? Do you believe that God called you to oversee the school and that the uninformed members of the board should not be directing you because of your training and experience? Of course, the response to several of these questions is the recognition of sin in your life—impatience, jealousy, rebellion, ambition.

Is your situation starting to feel like a pit? How about a prison? Now, call to your remembrance God's incredible plan and timetable for Joseph, who went from a pit, to a prison, to the pinnacle of the greatest nation on the earth—and eventually to the protection and nurturing of God's remnant, which would grow to become God's people in Egypt. Can you relax today and ask God to encourage you in what He has for you in the long run and in the meantime?

Board chair, are you struggling with the performance of the school's administrator? Have you considered that God has placed him or her in your care as a part of your stewardship? Is your goal to have peace and quiet, and as few interruptions as possible? Maybe the Lord needs you to participate in a season of carefully mentoring the school's leader. Give yourself to the work and include others who can help you share the load. Have you discovered that the administrator has inadequacies or sinful habits? If you have, you must speak with the leader thoughtfully and, if necessary, forcefully to clarify the situation and the relationship. Second, you must develop an improvement plan to enable this employee under your supervision either to improve over time or to realize clearly why his or her performance is not acceptable.

Maybe you lack training in this area; many consultants are available for assistance. Maybe you lack the courage to sit with someone and talk about painful issues face-to-face. Perhaps you imagine that it is easier to meet with a small group and dismiss your head of school, finding security in numbers. Are you intimidated? God will give you the words and the courage for this one-on-one meeting. Over the years I have met many leaders who were extremely successful and effective in a variety of settings but who lacked the skill of interpersonal relationship that enables a person in authority to have a conference with a subordinate and calmly work through difficult situations, particularly as they relate to the shortcomings of the subordinate. On the other hand, maybe you lack faith and cannot conceive of a person's actually changing his or her job performance. Maybe you have thought or said out loud, "He's too old to change," or "She wasn't born with it and just doesn't get it." May I encourage you to reconsider the parable of the talents, in which the Master rewards the faithful stewards by giving them more talents? Can the Holy Spirit not do a similar work in the administrator you are guiding?

I have chosen the words of Jeremiah from Lamentations 3:22–26 to close both this chapter and a book for those who must *navigate the storms*:

> The Lord's lovingkindnesses indeed never cease,
> > For His compassions never fail.
> They are new every morning;
> > Great is Your faithfulness.
> "The Lord is my portion," says my soul,
> > "Therefore I have hope in Him."
> The Lord is good to those who wait for Him,
> > To the person who seeks Him.
> It is good that he waits silently
> > For the salvation of the Lord.

Appendix

A NATIONWIDE FULL SERVICE CONFLICT MANAGEMENT FIRM

Mediation Law Group, Inc.™
Toll Free 1.866.403.8690   **Toll Free Fax 1.866.403.8693**

MEDIATION LAW GROUP™ RESOURCES
Sample Streamlined Contractual
Faith-Based Employment Dispute Resolution Program

The following is a sample Three-Step Employment Dispute Resolution Program for inclusion in a Christian organization's employment contracts. You are advised to seek independent legal advice from a qualified attorney as to the ramifications of including such alternate dispute resolution language in your contracts.

NOTE: If you incorporate these clauses into a contract, please advise
Mediation Law Group™ at 1-866-403-8690 or by email to admin@mediationlawgroup.com

Employer and employee recognize that Christians and Christian organizations are called by scripture to a different standard of resolving their differences (Matthew 18; 1 Corinthians 6). Resolving workplace disputes through processes alternate to the secular courts is often faster, more economical and confidential than the traditional court process, and tends to preserve relationships between the disputing parties. Therefore, in the event a dispute arises between the parties out of this agreement, or in the event any workplace dispute arises involving Employee, such dispute(s) shall be resolved through the following Streamlined Employment Dispute Resolution Program:

Step 1 - Employee shall first try to resolve the dispute internally, by discussing the matter informally with Employee's _____ (*i.e., department head, vice president, vice president of human resources, etc.*). If the dispute involves claims of sexual or workplace harassment, the informal resolution requirement set forth in this Step 1 shall *not* require Employee to interact with an alleged aggressor. Instead, Employer shall appoint another executive with decision-making authority to work with Employee to attempt to informally resolve the dispute at this Step 1 level. In the event disputes involving termination or legally-protected rights are not resolved through this Step 1 informal process, such disputes shall be required to go to Step 2, as provided below.

Step 2 - Employee and the parties to the dispute shall participate in mediation administered by the religious dispute division of Mediation Law Group™ (MLG), under its Mediation Rules. In the event settlement of the dispute does not occur at this stage, the parties may proceed to Step 3 (binding arbitration) at the option of Employee.

Step 3 - Employee, at employee's option, shall submit the dispute to binding arbitration administered by the religious dispute division of MLG, under its Employment Arbitration Rules, and judgment on the award rendered by the arbitrator(s) may be entered in any court having jurisdiction thereof.

In all instances (after Steps 1 and 2 have been exhausted by Employee), Employer shall be required to arbitrate the matter if Employee so elects under this provision. Should Employee elect to voluntarily submit to binding arbitration, Employer shall provide a one-time $1,000.00 reimbursement for Employee's (or former Employee's) attorney's fees for the mediation or arbitration of each matter. Additionally, all mediator and arbitrator expenses, unless the law provides to the contrary, shall be paid by Employer. Employee may, however, elect to pay up to one-half of the neutral's compensation and expenses.

The parties further acknowledge that where emergency interim relief is required by a party to this agreement, including but not limited to injunctive relief and orders for the protection or conservation of property and/or disposition of disposable goods, such relief may be granted by an MLG arbitrator upon application under the MLG Employment Arbitration Rules, even when the dispute is still in the Step 2 mediation phase. The parties acknowledge and agree that an application for such emergency interim relief shall not constitute a waiver or breach of mediation requirements under this provision.

IF ANY PARTY HERETO INITIATES AN ARBITRATION OR COURT PROCEEDINGS BASED UPON A DISPUTE TO WHICH THIS PROVISION APPLIES, WITHOUT FIRST PARTICIPATING IN STEPS 1 AND 2 ABOVE, THEN IN THE DISCRETION OF THE ARBITRATOR(S) OR JUDGE, SUCH PARTY SHALL NOT BE ENTITLED TO RECOVER ATTORNEYS' FEES, EVEN IF FEES WOULD OTHERWISE BE RECOVERABLE BY THAT PARTY IN ANY SUCH ARBITRATION OR COURT PROCEEDING.

MEDIATION LAW GROUP™ RESOURCES
Sample Streamlined Contractual
Faith-Based Employment Dispute Resolution Program
Page 2 of 2

163

References

Badertscher, Vera Marie. 2000–2001. King Gustavus goofed. *Renaissance Central* 1, no. 4 (December–January). http://www.rencentral.com/. Site now discontinued.

Barna, George. 1992. *The power of vision: How you can capture and apply God's vision for your ministry.* Ventura, CA: Regal Books.

Bathurst, Bella. 2005. *The wreckers: A story of killing seas and plundered shipwrecks, from the 18th century to the present day.* Boston: Houghton Mifflin.

Behring Center. *A brief history of lighthouses.* Smithsonian National Museum of American History. http://americanhistory.si.edu/collections/lighthouses/history.htm.

Blanchard, Ken, Bill Hybels, and Phil Hodges. 1999. *Leadership by the book: Tools to transform your workplace.* New York: William Morrow; Colorado Springs, CO: WaterBrook Press.

Blanchard, Ken, Patricia Zigarmi, and Drea Zigarmi. 1985. *Leadership and the one minute manager: Increasing effectiveness through situational leadership.* New York: William Morrow.

Brown, Gordon B. 2007–2008. The role of supervision in faculty development. *Christian School Education* 11, no. 3:22–24.

Carney, Burt. 2006. Can a student be expelled for having an inappropriate home website? *Legal/Legislative Update* 17, no. 1 (Fall): 18, 22–23.

———. 2007. Can a senior caught cheating be expelled just days before graduation? *Legal/Legislative Update* 18, no. 1 (Fall): 16, 21–22.

———, ed. 2009. *Personnel resources for Christian schools.* CD. Colorado Springs, CO: Purposeful Design Publications.

Christian Law Association. 2006. *Cell phone use.* Seminole, FL: Christian Law Association.

Clinton, J. Robert. 1988. *The making of a leader: Recognizing the lessons and stages of leadership development.* Colorado Springs, CO: NavPress.

Coley, Kenneth S. 1998. How Southern Baptists do Christian schooling. *Facts and Trends,* January–February:11.

———. 2006. *The helmsman: Leading with courage and wisdom.* Colorado Springs, CO: Purposeful Design Publications.

Cookman, Scott. 2000. *Ice blink: The tragic fate of Sir John Franklin's lost polar expedition.* New York: John Wiley and Sons.

Cousins, Don. 1990. Overseeing staff. In *Mastering church management,* by Leith Anderson, Don Cousins, and Arthur DeKruyter, 137–50. Portland, OR: Multnomah Press.

Csorba, Les T. 2004. *Trust: The one thing that makes or breaks a leader.* Nashville, TN: Thomas Nelson.

Curtis, Richard K. 1962. *They called him Mister Moody.* Garden City, NY: Doubleday.

Davidson, Bill. 1998–1999. Ten commandments for school board members. *Christian School Education* 2, no. 2:10.

Department of Geological Sciences. How volcanoes work: Krakatau, Indonesia (1883). San Diego State University College of Sciences. http://www.geology.sdsu.edu/how_volcanoes_work/Krakatau.html.

Dictionary of Canadian Biography Online. 2000. S.v. "Franklin, Sir John" (by University of Toronto). http://www.biographi.ca/009004-119.01-e.php?BioId=37516 (accessed March 11, 2010).

Discovery Channel. 2006. *Krakatoa: Volcano of destruction.* Dramatized television documentary.

Downey, Carolyn J., Betty E. Steffy, Fenwick W. English, Larry E. Frase, and William K. Poston Jr. 2004. *The three-minute classroom walk-through: Changing school supervisory practice one teacher at a time.* Thousand Oaks, CA: Corwin Press.

Drexler, James L. 2007–2008. Why is community so vital for Christian schools? Review of *Schools as communities,* ed. James L. Drexler. *Christian School Education* 11, no. 1:13.

Feinberg, Ted, and Nicole Robey. 2008. Cyberbullying. *Principal Leadership* 9, no. 1 (September): 10–14.

Gangel, Kenneth O. 1997. *Team leadership in Christian ministry: Using multiple gifts to build a unified vision.* Rev. ed. Chicago: Moody Press.

———. 2005–2006. A rose by any other name: What is integrity? *Christian School Education* 9, convention special:5–8.

———. 2008. *Surviving toxic leaders: How to work for flawed people in churches, schools, and Christian organizations.* Eugene, OR: Wipf and Stock.

Gibbs Law Firm. 2010. *Internet threats.* Seminole, FL: Christian Law Association.

Goering, Janeal. 2006–2007. Review of *Overcoming the five dysfunctions of a team,* by Patrick Lencioni. *Christian School Education* 10, no. 4:15.

Great Britain, Parliament, Commons. 2009. *Abridgment of the minutes of the evidence, taken before a committee of the whole house: To whom it was referred to consider of the slave-trade, 1789.* General Books LLC.

Greenleaf, Robert K. 2002. *Servant leadership: A journey into the nature of legitimate power and greatness.* 25th anniversary ed. Ed. Larry C. Spears. New York: Paulist Press.

Grose, Francis. 1971. *1811 dictionary of the vulgar tongue: A dictionary of buckish slang, university wit, and pickpocket eloquence.* Pleasantville, NY: Digest Books.

Guthrie, Donald. 1983. *The letter to the Hebrews: An introduction and commentary.* Tyndale New Testament Commentaries. Grand Rapids, MI: Wm. B. Eerdmans Publishing; Leicester, England: InterVarsity Press.

Haddock, Jerry L. 2002. Navigating the maze: Coping with constant change. In *Called to lead: Understanding and fulfilling your role as an educational leader,* ed. Kenneth O. Gangel, 271–86. Colorado Springs, CO: Purposeful Design Publications.

Heck, Ronald H. 1992. Principals' instructional leadership and school performance: Implications for policy development. *Educational Evaluation and Policy Analysis* 14, no. 1 (Spring): 21–34.

Hill, Christopher. 1987. *The collected essays of Christopher Hill,* vol. 1, *Writing and revolution in 17th century England.* Amherst: University of Massachusetts Press.

Hopkins, Gary. 2009. Walk-throughs are on the move. *Education World,* July 23. http://www.educationworld.com/a_admin/admin/admin405.shtml.

John Paul Jones Museum. Life of John Paul Jones. John Paul Jones Birthplace Museum Trust. http://www.jpj.demon.co.uk/jpjlife.htm.

Johnson, Scott, and Dave Edgren. 2006–2007. Is the book *The five dysfunctions of a team* consistent with Scripture? *Christian School Education* 10, no. 3:14.

Jones, Ray. 1995. *Southern lighthouses: Chesapeake Bay to the Gulf of Mexico.* 2nd ed. With photographs by Bruce Roberts. Old Saybrook, CT: Globe Pequot Press.

Junger, Sebastian. 1997. *The perfect storm: A true story of men against the sea.* New York: W. W. Norton.

Kittel, Gerhard, and Gerhard Friedrich, eds. 1985. *Theological dictionary of the New Testament.* Abridged ed. Trans. Geoffrey W. Bromiley. Grand Rapids, MI: William B. Eerdmans Publishing.

Kotter, John, and Holger Rathgeber. 2005. *Our iceberg is melting: Changing and succeeding under any conditions.* New York: St. Martin's Press.

Lavery, Brian. 2003. *Horatio Lord Nelson.* The British Library Historic Lives Series. New York: New York University Press.

Lencioni, Patrick. 2002. *The five dysfunctions of a team: A leadership fable.* San Francisco, CA: Jossey-Bass.

Lockerbie, D. Bruce. 2007. *A passion for learning: A history of Christian thought on education.* Colorado Springs, CO: Purposeful Design Publications.

———. 2007–2008. First things first: What makes Christian schooling distinctive? *Christian School Education* 11, no. 1:5–8.

Lowrie, Roy W., Jr., and Roy L. Lowrie. 2004. *Serving God on the Christian school board.* 3rd ed. Colorado Springs, CO: Purposeful Design Publications.

Lundgren, Michelle. 2007–2008. A dangerous complacency. *Christian School Education* 11, no. 1:9–12.

Miller, Frederic P., Agnes F. Vandome, and John McBrewster, eds. 2009. *Impressment.* Beau Bassin, Mauritius: Alphascript Publishing.

Moore, Richard. 1999a. Demands of the Nore mutineers. Napoleonic Guide. http://www.napoleonguide.com/navy-nore-articles.htm.

———. 1999b. Mutiny at Spithead. Napoleonic Guide. http://www.napoleonguide.com/navy_spithead.htm.

———. 1999c. Mutiny at the Nore. Napoleonic Guide. http://www.napoleonguide.com/navy_nore.htm.

Nason, Janet Lowrie. 2002. Protecting your quiddity: Emphasizing Christian school uniqueness. In *Called to lead: Understanding and fulfilling your role as an educational leader,* ed. Kenneth O. Gangel, 1–16. Colorado Springs, CO: Purposeful Design Publications.

Naval Historical Center. 2003. Traditions of the naval service: Striking the flag. Naval History and Heritage Command. http://www.history.navy.mil/trivia/trivia03-1.htm.

NHC. See Naval Historical Center.

North Raleigh Christian Academy Administration, comp. 2009. *North Raleigh Christian Academy parent/student handbook.* July 23 revision. Ed. Sonny L. Sherrill. Raleigh, NC: North Raleigh Christian Academy.

NRCA Administration. *See* North Raleigh Christian Academy Administration.

O'Neill, Richard. 2003. *Patrick O'Brian's navy: The illustrated companion to Jack Aubrey's world.* Philadelphia, PA: Running Press.

Philbrick, Nathaniel. 2006. *Mayflower: A story of courage, community, and war.* New York: Penguin Books.

Reuters. 2003. Krakatoa provided backdrop to Munch's *Scream.* The Age. December 11. http://www.theage.com.au. Web page now discontinued.

References

Riesen, Richard A. 2006–2007. Teachers, mission statements, and "education's larger purposes." *Christian School Education* 10, no. 3:40–41.

Schimmer, John. 1998–1999. Parents on the school board. *Christian School Education* 2, no. 4:32.

Schindler, Claude E., Jr. 1979. *Education for eternity.* With Pacheco Pyle. Wheaton, IL: Tyndale House.

─────. 1987. *Sowing for excellence: Educating God's way.* With Pacheco Pyle. Whittier, CA: Association of Christian Schools International.

Sergiovanni, Thomas J. 1992. *Moral leadership: Getting to the heart of school improvement.* San Francisco, CA: Jossey-Bass.

─────. 1995. *The principalship: A reflective practice perspective.* 3rd ed. Boston: Allyn and Bacon.

Sheppard, Jeffrey C. 2006–2007. Cyberbullying: An emerging threat to our students. *Christian School Education* 10, no. 3:44–45.

Smith, Alfred B. 1985. *Al Smith's treasury of hymn histories: The authentic, inspiring, and often unknown stories behind the writing of over 115 favorite hymns and gospel songs.* Greenville, SC: Better Music Publications.

Stronks, Gloria Goris, and Doug Blomberg, eds. 1993. *A vision with a task: Christian schooling for responsive discipleship.* Grand Rapids, MI: Baker Books.

Sweet, Leonard I. 1999. *AquaChurch: Essential leadership arts for piloting your church in today's fluid culture.* Loveland, CO: Group Publishing.

Swindoll, Charles R. 1978. *Hand me another brick.* Nashville, TN: Thomas Nelson.

Uecker, Milton V. 2007–2008. The significance of education. *Christian School Education* 11, no. 1:14–16.

Vasa Museum. n.d.a. The disaster. Vasa Museum. http://www.vasamuseet.se/sitecore/content/ Vasamuseet/InEnglish/History/disaster.aspx. Web page now discontinued.

─────. n.d.b. *Vasa*—an art treasure. Vasa Museum. http://www.vasamuseet.se/sitecore/ content/Vasamuseet/InEnglish/History/art.aspx. Web page now discontinued.

─────. n.d.c. Why did *Vasa* sink? Vasa Museum. http://www.vasamuseet.se/sitecore/ content/Vasamuseet/InEnglish/History/why.aspx. Web page now discontinued.

WB-Sails. 1998. Telling tales. WB-Sails. http://www.wb-sails.fi/news/95_11_Tellingtales/ Tellingtales.html.

Weir, Peter, and John Collee. 2003. *Master and commander.* Movie. Directed by Peter Weir. Los Angeles, CA: Twentieth-Century Fox.

Wilkes, C. Gene. 1998. *Jesus on leadership: Discovering the secrets of servant leadership from the life of Christ.* Wheaton, IL: Tyndale House.

Williamson, H. G. M. 1985. *Ezra, Nehemiah.* Vol. 16 of *Word biblical commentary,* gen. ed. David A. Hubbard and Glenn W. Barker. Waco, TX: Word Books.

Wright, David, and David Zoby. 2000. *Fire on the beach: Recovering the lost story of Richard Etheridge and the Pea Island lifesavers.* New York: Oxford University Press.

Young, Robert. n.d. *Young's Analytical Concordance to the Bible.* Peabody, MA: Hendrickson.

Zepeda, Sally J. 2005. *The instructional leader's guide to informal classroom observations.* Larchmont, NY: Eye on Education.